High in Utah

Alaska is our biggest, buggiest, boggiest state. Texas remains our largest unfrozen state. But mountainous Utah, if ironed out flat, would take up more space on a map than either.

—Edward Abbey, 1927–1989

High in Utah

A Hiking Guide to the Tallest Peak
in Each of the State's Twenty-nine Counties

Michael R. Weibel and Dan Miller

University of Utah Press
Salt Lake City, Utah

Library of Congress Cataloging-in-Publication Data

Weibel, Michael R., 1964–
    High in Utah : a hiking guide to the tallest summits in the state's
twenty-nine counties / Michael R. Weibel and Dan Miller.
        p.   cm.
    Includes bibliographical references.
    ISBN-10: 0-87480-588-0   ISBN-13: 978-0-87480-588-8
    1. Mountaineering–Utah–Guidebooks. 2. Trails–Utah–Guidebooks.
3. Utah–Guidebooks.   I. Miller, Dan, 1954–   . II. Title.
GV199.42.U8W45   1999
917.9204'33–dc21   98-45959

Cartography and book design by Dan Miller

In memory of

Gladys Naomi (Mullins) Weibel, 1940–1990

and

Ginny Dean Holmes, 1946–1996

Contents

County High Peaks

Utah Classics

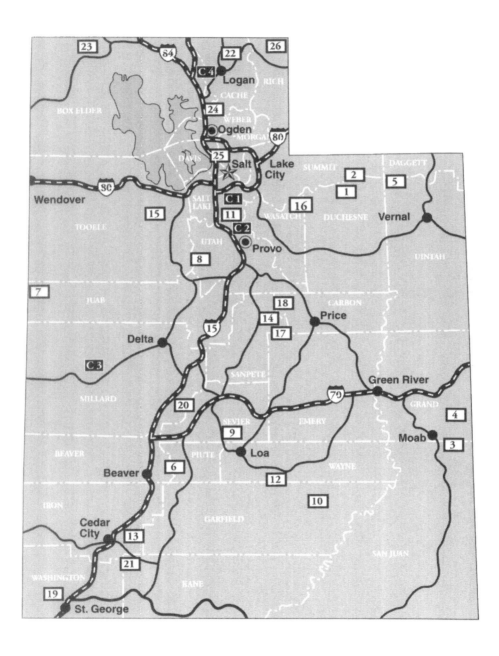

MOUNTAIN ✔ CHECKLIST

☐ 1 KINGS PEAK, 13,528', Duchesne County

☐ 2 GILBERT PEAK, 13,442', Summit County

☐ 3 MOUNT PEALE, 12,721', San Juan County

☐ 4 MOUNT WAAS, 12,331', Grand County

☐ 5 ECCENTRIC PEAK, 12,276', Daggett & Uintah Counties

☐ 6 DELANO PEAK, 12,169', Beaver & Piute Counties

☐ 7 IBAPAH PEAK, 12,087', Juab County

☐ 8 MOUNT NEBO, 11,928', Utah County

☐ 9 FISH LAKE HIGHTOP, 11,633', Sevier County

☐ 10 MOUNT ELLEN, 11,522', Garfield County

☐ 11 AMERICAN FORK TWIN PEAKS, 11,489', Salt Lake County

☐ 12 BLUEBELL KNOLL, 11,328', Wayne County

☐ 13 BRIAN HEAD PEAK, 11,307', Iron County

☐ 14 SOUTH TENT MOUNTAIN, 11,285', Sanpete County

☐ 15 DESERET PEAK, 11,031', Tooele County

☐ 16 UNNAMED, 10,743', Wasatch County

☐ 17 EAST MOUNTAIN, 10,743', Emery County

☐ 18 MONUMENT PEAK, 10,452', Carbon County

☐ 19 SIGNAL PEAK, 10,365', Washington County

☐ 20 MINE CAMP PEAK, 10,222', Millard County

☐ 21 UNNAMED, 10,027', Kane County

☐ 22 NAOMI PEAK, 9,979', Cache County

☐ 23 BULL MOUNTAIN, 9,934', Box Elder County

☐ 24 WILLARD PEAK, 9,763', Weber County

☐ 25 THURSTON PEAK, 9,706', Davis & Morgan Counties

☐ 26 UNNAMED, 9,255', Rich County

☐ C1 MOUNT OLYMPUS, 9,026', A UTAH CLASSIC

☐ C2 MOUNT TIMPANOGOS, 11,749', A UTAH CLASSIC

☐ C3 NOTCH PEAK, 9,654', A UTAH CLASSIC

☐ C4 WELLSVILLE CONE, 9,356', A UTAH CLASSIC

ASPEN UNDER MOUNT NEBO

Preface

In the summer of 1996, I was chatting with Cache County Attorney Scott Wyatt about half a dozen things—some legal stuff, some mountains. We had climbed together a year or so earlier in the Cascades and were anxious to get out of our offices and tackle another climb.

Scott pulled out a copy of *The Salt Lake Tribune* from July 1995 that featured a map of the highest peak in each of the state's twenty-nine counties. The paper told of an ambitious undertaking by writer Paula Huff to climb each of the peaks. The project was, in part, to celebrate Utah's Centennial in 1996.

It sounded like a good idea.

I mulled the idea over for a few days. Then something clicked. Why not write a guidebook detailing each of the peaks? If we could sell the idea to a publisher, we could get paid to do something we love—climbing mountains all summer.

I called photojournalist Dan Miller, a friend since I moved to Utah in 1992. He had dragged me out on my first Utah hike, in Logan Canyon, just after I started working at *The Herald Journal*. Since then, we had done a lot of hiking, climbing, and skiing together. He liked the idea and we jumped right to work. It didn't take much arm twisting to convince Jeff Grathwohl at the University of Utah Press to buy the idea. He, too, is a climber. He loved the idea, even before he looked at the samples we had put together featuring Naomi and Willard peaks.

We were on our way, but there was one problem: we both despised guidebooks.

One of the benefits of venturing outdoors in Utah is that you can get away from the hustle and bustle of work, get away from the crowds, and share in the beauty and delight that Mother Nature provides. You can see wildflowers in a high Alpine meadow, smell the aromatic pines, and witness a bull moose browsing in a forest. It's nature and the outdoors, the very basics of life on earth.

But as Utah's unprecedented growth pushes cities beyond their boundaries in a frenzied state of panic, a guidebook seems destined only to spoil Utah's wilderness. Scores of modern-day adventurers could be led by a guidebook into the mountains where they would trample the wildflowers, pollute the air with odd smells and noises, and chase the animals away. Ed Abbey would be appalled.

But it was too late. We had already sold out our love of the wilderness to put together a book. Between May 25 and October 5, 1997, we climbed twenty-three of the peaks together (Naomi, Willard, and Unnamed Rich

County were already behind us). We put more than 7,000 miles on our trucks. Dan climbed 84,172 feet in elevation and hiked 267.5 miles, including the four "classics" in this book. I climbed 62,299 feet in elevation and hiked 210.5 miles.

We had to justify why we were putting out a guidebook. We had to find a way to make it right. I think we succeeded.

While we were busy hiking in the summer of 1997, Huff's series of newspaper articles was reprinted in the book *Hiking Utah's Summits*. Soon after, Michael Kelsey's decade-old book *Utah Mountaineering Guide* was updated and reprinted. It was inevitable that people would soon be flocking to Utah's county high peaks with either of those books or with photocopies of Huff's original newspaper articles.

Dan and I tried to improve upon those books, focusing specifically on the directions to trailheads and summits while leaving out long explanations of the history and background of each mountain. We purposely described only one route to the top of each mountain so Forest Service officials and other land managers can concentrate their maintenance efforts on the most-used routes. We have also emphasized the importance of low impact hiking and camping, the preservation of wilderness, and—as Dan points out—an appreciation of wildness.

—Mike Weibel

... this tameness (of wilderness) is exacerbated by our current
model for appropriate human use of the wild—the intensive
recreation that requires trail systems, bridges, signs for direction and distance, backcountry rangers, and rescue operations
that in turn generate activities that further diminish wildness
—maps, guide books, guiding services, advertising, photography books, instructional films—all of which diminish the
discovery, surprise, the unknown, and the often dangerous
Other—the very qualities that make a place wild. Each of
these reductions tames and domesticates the wilderness and
diminishes wild experience.

—Jack Turner, *The Abstract Wild*

Why am I participating in a guidebook? How can I justify producing something that could diminish or tame wildness, which I love? These questions lin-
gered, humming a little song of guilt during the entire production of this book.
I tried to ignore the song, hoping it would go away. When I couldn't quash the
notes, I attempted to answer the questions with personal justifications.

The first justification jumped to mind. I've lived in Utah, a state I love, for
thirty-three years. I've been hiking Utah for most of that time, and I know
there are still many places I've never visited. This project allowed me, even
required me, to travel to places I never had a reason to visit before. How could
I refuse?

Other justifications came a little more slowly. The routes listed in this book
are not new, and they are not secret. People in the communities nearby have
traveled them for years. So I'm not giving anything away. How could I refuse?

Other guidebooks already include several of these routes with flawed or
outdated descriptions. By correcting past mistakes, this guidebook might help
prevent people from getting lost or hurt. That, in turn, could reduce the number of rescue operations that further diminish wildness. And isn't a guidebook
in the hands of a hiker much less intrusive to the sense of wildness than trail
signs posted at every turn? How could I refuse?

The humming behind my ear hasn't stopped. These justifications are not
valid. The truth remains; no matter what rationalizations I can create, this
book will diminish the experience of wildness. And you, as a reader, validate
that process.

Why are we human beings so attracted to high places? Where does our
desire to get to the lip of outer space and gaze into the beyond come from? I
have no answers. I only know that I'm magnetically drawn to the highest
points. A ridge I haven't peered over or a summit blocking my view always
pulls me to the top, where I can look at the world around me and be humbled
by my insignificance. At the same time, I can look toward infinity with no

obstructions and dream. The fact that so many of us feel this desire is part of the problem that Turner describes.

The highest point within a political boundary possesses even more magnetism. For example, the highest point within the political boundaries of Utah is Kings Peak, whose boulder summit is by no means extraordinary. Yet a never-ending swarm of hikers making their way to this high point has created what I call the "King's Highway." Their numbers alone are enough to destroy the wildness of this place.

Although I have hiked high summits throughout the western United States, I have never considered myself a peak bagger. For me, the summits were always an excuse to travel and hike new terrain. But working on deadline for this book made our timing from peak to peak crucial. We never had time to spend in an area to explore beyond our primary goal, the high summit. We became the definitive peak baggers. In retrospect, I realize my goal of experiencing the wild places of Utah was truly diminished.

So here is my challenge to you readers. Use this guidebook to find your way to the high peaks of Utah. Once you have completed the hike and returned to the car, put the book under the seat and leave the maps in the glove box. Feel free to take off on a feeling, a whim, a fancy. Follow your nose. Sense the breeze blowing in from the meadow ahead. Skirt the perimeter and follow the elk tracks into the next hollow. Hear the Golden Eagle shout directions and answer its voice with a screech of thanks. Don't forget to taste the mist floating from the waterfall you have just discovered. And, if you are very lucky, maybe you will feel the burning eyes of a cougar on the back of your neck and experience "the unknown, and the often dangerous" qualities of the wild.

When you return home with the experience of wildness in your heart, begin to pursue the world we live in with a new vigor. Take the experience and turn it into an effort to restore the wildness we have lost and to save what little we still have.

Dan Miller

—Dan Miller

Caution

Climbing and hiking in Utah is inherently dangerous. All participants in such activities must assume the responsibility for their own actions and safety. The information contained in this guidebook cannot replace sound judgment, good decision-making skills, and experience, which help reduce the exposure to risk.

This book does not attempt to disclose all of the potential hazards involved in such activities. You should not depend on any information gleaned from this book for personal safety. Your safety depends on your own good judgment, based on experience and a realistic assessment of your abilities and prevailing conditions surrounding them. If you have any doubt as to your ability to safely hike any of the routes described in this book, do not attempt them.

This book is not a substitute for instruction and experience. Learn as much as possible about climbing and hiking in Utah before venturing into the mountains. Prepare for the unexpected and be cautious.

Neither the authors nor the publisher are responsible for the reader's safety.

How to Use This Book

This book doesn't waste pages telling stories about the people who worked and inhabited Utah's high mountains. Instead, it is a book designed for peak baggers—people who want to climb the highest peaks in each of Utah's twenty-nine counties. It's that simple: no frills, just enough information to get someone from the trailhead to the summit.

Our book places a particular emphasis on the directions to each trailhead. Many guidebooks seem to ignore the importance of getting to the right place to start a hike, and nothing can be more frustrating than getting lost before even getting on the mountain.

There are numerous ways to get to many of the trailheads. But, for simplicity, most directions are given from nearby cities or Interstate 15, as if the reader is approaching from Salt Lake City. We recommend a good road map, which the Utah Department of Transportation gives away free. In 1987, the Utah Travel Council put out a series of five good Utah Multipurpose Maps covering the state, but a full set may be difficult to find.

We made every effort to ensure the accuracy of the instructions. The routes described in this book are not always the easiest or most practical ways to reach the summits. We chose them because they appealed to us and also because they have been commonly cited in previous guidebooks.

As we have already emphasized, we hope the increased visits to Utah's county high peaks will be confined to these traditional routes so land managers such as the Forest Service can concentrate their maintenance efforts on them.

Early chapters in this guide are devoted to low impact camping and hiking and to Utah's wilderness areas. We hope that people who use this book will abide by the "Leave No Trace" practices to help ensure that generations of backcountry users can continue to have wonderful experiences in Utah's beautiful mountains.

Times

Each mountain chapter provides two guidelines for the time it takes to reach the summit of each peak and return to the trailhead. These times are represented by the symbols of a tortoise and a hare.

People hike at different speeds. Mike is the larger and significantly slower hiker of the two of us. His times are displayed as the faster end of the range portrayed by the tortoise (see example). Dan, who is the smaller and quicker hiker, kept track of time using a stopwatch. He often hiked well ahead of Mike and, when he stopped at a landmark or trail junction, would keep track of the time it took for Mike to catch up. At the end of the hike, we deducted the stopwatch time from Mike's overall time to give Dan's approximate time—depicted as the slower end of the range indicated by the hare.

Time: 7–8 hours 4–5.5 hours

Contrary to the fable, the tortoise never beat the hare, but he tied a few times on the easiest mountains.

Distances

The distances mentioned in each mountain chapter are round trip. Because several sources provided conflicting mileage figures for many of the mountains, the distances were often calculated based on books, signs, and maps. Although no mileage can be completely accurate, we made every effort to avoid errors.

Difficulty

We rated each mountain as *too easy, easy, moderate, difficult,* or *extreme.* The criteria for the ratings were borrowed, in part, from *Canyon Country's La Sal Mountains Hiking and Nature Handbook* by José Knighton. The ratings are quite subjective and are intended only as suggestions to help during preparations before the hike.

- *Too Easy* peaks are those reached by car.
- *Easy* routes are generally along developed trails and less than six miles round trip.
- *Moderate* routes might include less developed trails and perhaps some off-trail route-finding. This category also includes hikes longer than six miles on established trails. Elevation gain may be a factor on some moderate hikes.
- *Difficult* routes are long and include significant elevation gain. Off-trail route-finding is also likely.
- *Extreme* routes are long and steep, often with scree, talus, and boulders that must be negotiated—sometimes requiring hands as well as feet. There may not be any kind of trail for significant portions of the routes and help, if necessary, may be difficult to come by. Only experienced hikers should attempt these mountains.

Tips and Precautions

Most of the routes described in this book have unique aspects that hikers should be aware of before they attempt the climbs. While we developed these tips and precautions through our own personal experiences, others may encounter different conditions that may warrant further cautions. Remember the Boy Scout motto and "be prepared" for any situation when venturing outdoors in Utah.

Maps

Of course you should consult a U.S. Geological Survey topographic map before each hike. The maps in this book are based on USGS maps, and all of the geographic names and elevations are taken from those maps. Contour lines are shown to give readers an idea of where ridges and drainages are located.

The scales for the maps in this book vary. One inch on one map, for example, represents different mileage than one inch on another map.

Our maps are not as detailed as the USGS maps. However, we noticed changes since some of the USGS maps were made, and we have attempted to show roads, trails, and landmarks as they appeared in 1997.

After reviewing the USGS map, hikers will determine from their own personal experience and judgment if a more detailed map than the one in this book is necessary equipment to carry along. We recommend a compass and some kind of map for every hike.

USGS maps can be purchased in many outdoor equipment stores, as well as at many state and federal agencies including Forest Service offices and the Utah Geologic Survey. USGS maps are also available to read and copy, for a modest cost, in libraries at most of the state's colleges, Brigham Young University, and the Salt Lake City public library.

Trails Illustrated also publishes a line of topographic maps, primarily for the Uintas and the national parks in Utah.

Camping

The camping information listed with many of the mountains is based on the U.S. Forest Service publication *Camping and Picnicking in the National Forests of Utah*. Fees, amenities, and other information were accurate as of 1997.

Photographs

Miller draped two cameras, weighing a total of fifteen pounds, around his neck for most of the hikes in this book. He used primarily a Nikon 8008 camera with a 35–70 mm lens and Kodak T-Max 100 black and white film, and a Leica M6 camera with Fuji Velvia color slide film.

Thanks go out to the dozens of people who joined us on the various hikes throughout the state. Kevin Brewer, Diane Bush, Scott Dunn, Mark Elzey, Stanley Holmes, Wesley Holmes, José Knighton, Kandi Kutkas, Marlin Stum, Rory Tyler, and S. John Wilkin to name a few. Unfortunately, through the editing process not everyone's picture could be included.

Introduction

For people flying into Salt Lake City, the sight of the mountains of the Wasatch towering over Utah's capital can be an unforgettable first impression.

Utah's mountains are not the Himalayas, but by one standard they are the highest in the country. According to a series of stories that ran in *The Salt Lake Tribune*, the average elevation of Utah's tallest peaks in each county is roughly 11,222 feet. Colorado ranks second, with an average county high peak elevation of 10,791 feet, followed by Nevada (10,764 feet) and Wyoming (10,179 feet). Alaska, home to the country's highest peak—the 20,320-foot Denali—ranks only sixth, with an average county high peak elevation of 9,280 feet.

Most of Utah's county high peaks grow out of a series of mountain ranges that form a backbone of sorts running through the middle of the state: from the Pine Valley Mountains near St. George, to the Pavants and Tushars east of Richfield, along the Wasatch Plateau to the Wasatch Mountains east of the state's largest cities, to the Bear River Mountains running north from Cache Valley into Idaho.

The state's highest peak, Kings Peak (13,528 feet), is found in the Uinta Mountains, which run east from the Wasatch range—one of only a few major east-west ranges in the world. The Himalayas, home to the highest peak on earth, Mount Everest, is another.

Alone in the western part of the state is Ibapah, in the Deep Creek Mountains, rising above the surrounding desert to more than 12,000 feet above sea level. Deseret Peak is also alone, overseeing the Great Salt Lake from the Stansbury Mountains.

Mount Waas and Mount Peale are sisters of sorts in the La Sal Mountains above Moab, while Mount Ellen stands proudly over Capitol Reef National Park in the Henry Mountains—the last group of mountains to be named and mapped in the contiguous forty-eight states.

Surprisingly, most of these mountains can be climbed in one day. In fact, some summits can be reached in a car. Getting to the tops of the rest involves hiking, not climbing in its technical sense. Although technical climbing equipment such as ropes, ice axes, or crampons is not usually used for reaching these summits, such equipment may be necessary depending on the conditions. Proper training and experience in hiking and climbing are essential.

Peak-bagging is becoming more and more popular in Utah, but we hope readers will take their time and enjoy the natural surroundings unique to each peak. Several peaks would make good weekend destinations for family outings, while others would provide challenges unsurpassed in the West.

Flora and Fauna of Utah's Mountains

Most of Utah's county high peaks reach into two general elevation zones. The first zone, the Hudsonian or sub-Alpine life zone, spans roughly 9,000 feet to timberline. The second zone, the Alpine life zone, is approximately 11,000 feet and above. Most of the hikes, however, begin at lower elevations.

As hikers approach a mountain in Utah, the first zone they will likely encounter is the transition life zone at 7,000 to 8,000 feet. The next is the Canadian life zone, roughly between 8,000 and 9,000 feet.

The transition life zone is generally in the foothills. It is characterized by grasses and sagebrush at the lower margins, overtaken by mountain brush higher up. Some of the trees and woody shrubs that dominate in this zone include Gambel oak, pinyon pine, Utah

MOUNTAIN MAHOGANY

juniper, and mountain mahogany, as well as bigtooth maple in the wetter drainages. Alder, river birch, and cottonwood can also be found in riparian areas. Higher up in this life zone, you may see ponderosa, or yellow pine. Bitterbrush, milkvetch, balsam root, showy goldeneye, and silky lupine are just a few of the shrub and bloomers at these elevations.

Black-tailed jackrabbits, cottontails, red fox, coyote, mule deer, desert bighorn sheep, and Rocky Mountain elk inhabit the transition life zone, as do moose, black bear, and mountain lion. Ruffed grouse, scrub and Steller's jays, juncos, and hummingbirds also make this elevation their home. Most snakes such as gopher, bull, and garter snakes are harmless, but it is not uncommon to find a western or timber rattlesnake living in this life zone.

Climbing higher, hikers will cross into the Canadian life zone. Here are found many of the same tree species as in the transition life zone plus Douglas fir—probably the most common tree in this life zone. Even higher, you will likely run across limber and lodgepole pines, white fir, blue spruce, and quaking aspen. In the wetter drainages you will find big tooth maple, alder, river birch, and dogwood, a shrub with distinctive red bark. Other shrubby plants in this life zone include elderberry, currant, mountain ash, chokecherry, willow, and mountain lilac. Mountain bluebell, cinquefoil, columbine, violet and penstemon will also show their colors.

Elk and deer thrive at these elevations during the summer and fall, but rarely move higher. Smaller animals such as the cottontail, Uinta ground squirrel, yellow belly marmot, pika, and squirrel love this environment and make a good meal for a great horned owl or red-tailed hawk. Flickers, a variety of wrens, finches, and the distinctive mountain chickadee make their summer home here, where a bug supply is usually ample. It is not uncommon to spot a brilliant western tanager or a western bluebird dashing across an open meadow. Hummingbirds buzz about the wildflowers like bees during the peak wildflower season up high.

The short growing season and exposure to constant wind and weather are generally evident among trees and plants in the Hudsonian life zone. Engelmann spruce, sub-Alpine fir, and limber and bristlecone pines are hardy enough to stake their ground, but they rarely reach their full size. Bristlecones, the longest-living tree species on earth, are found only in the Great Basin region of Utah, Arizona, Nevada, and California.

Hikers may spot the showy pink blossoms of Parry's primrose, elephant's head, and shooting star around marshy spots in this sub-Alpine zone. High mountain sage, columbine, sticky geranium, paintbrush, and lupine prefer the drier meadows.

A wide variety of insects, rodents, and visiting birds will inhabit this life zone for a short time during the summer months, but almost all beat a hasty retreat to lower elevations when autumn nears. Pikas are one of the hardiest residents of this life zone. You can often see them dashing about the rocks and scree fields of the higher basins collecting plants and grasses that will serve as their home and food source through the winter.

Many of Utah's county high peaks reach into the Alpine life zone. Plant life that can withstand the harsh conditions at these elevations includes only a small selection of grasses, mosses, sedges, and lichens. A few hardy annuals bloom for a few weeks in sheltered spots this high, where it can freeze or snow year-round.

You might find a few birds and rodents up here, but most critters will keep to the lower elevations where life is considerably easier.

—Adapted from information provided by Bicycle Utah Vacation Guides, Inc.

Mountain Weather

by William J. Alder
Chief Meteorologist, National Weather Service, Salt Lake City

Hiking, climbing, and camping in the mountainous areas of the state are some of the ways outdoor vacationers can enjoy the many beauties of Utah. Weather conditions determine when and where vacationers go and the type of activities that are safe.

Winter conditions commence in some of the higher elevations as early as mid-September and last until mid-June. However, the main accumulation of snowfall is from November to April. In some of the higher mountain ranges of the state (above 10,000 feet), snow can persist throughout the summer on the north-facing slopes. As the snow melts in the spring/early summer, water feeds the streams, rivers, and reservoirs throughout

MIKE WRINGS RAINWATER FROM HIS SOCKS

the state. Snowmelt is the main source of water for this, the second driest state in the nation.

Weather is an important force of nature, and it should be respected. If you plan to enjoy the great outdoors, you should have a general idea of the weather. In the mountains the air is thin and temperatures drop rapidly as soon as the sun sets. A general rule of thumb is that daytime temperatures are about five degrees Fahrenheit cooler per 1,000 feet of elevation gained. Nighttime temperatures can vary a great deal depending on whether you are in a lower valley, on the side of a mountain, or in a forested area. It's not unusual to experience freezing temperatures during the summer months at elevations of 9,000 feet or higher.

Late summer and early fall snowfalls are not uncommon. Generally, high elevations can intensify storm conditions. An increase in clouds, wind speed, and change in wind direction are the usual signs that a weather system is approaching.

Thunderstorms and associated lightning are a major concern for outdoor enthusiasts from May through October. Lightning produced by the thunderheads can be beautiful, but deadly. Lightning is Utah's number one weather-related killer. Since 1954, lightning in Utah has caused 45 deaths and 102 injuries.

On warm summer days, the sun's rays heat the mountain slopes and puffy cumulus clouds begin to form. In the late morning to early afternoon, these clouds can grow into thunderheads. These tall cumulonimbus clouds typically have a dark, sometimes flat, black bottom and anvil-shaped tops. They signal that a thunderstorm is imminent.

In the past century, lightning has taken the lives of several Scouts in the Uinta Mountains. A Scout excursion on August 2, 1991, for example, turned to tragedy around noon when a fast-moving thunderstorm passed over the Scouts' camp located at the 10,700-foot level in a primitive area of the Uinta National Forest. Four boys took refuge under a pine tree. As one of them walked out from underneath the limbs, a bolt of lightning struck the tree, killing two boys aged fourteen and sixteen, and injuring the others.

July 18, 1997, turned deadly for a fifty-two-year-old Scout leader from Bountiful who was struck and killed by lightning. He and four others were returning to their camp at Henrys Fork Lake from fishing at Cliff Lake (11,400 feet) in the Uinta Mountains when a thunderstorm hit. Another Scout leader and a Scout were knocked unconscious by the lightning bolt and both of them sustained minor injuries.

Be prepared to move to cover if a storm is nearby. If you see lightning and hear thunder within a few seconds, seek shelter immediately. Once a storm is nearby and has begun, remember the "flash-to-bang" method to calculate how close it is: when you see the flash, count the seconds to the bang, then divide by five (i.e., ten seconds means it is two miles away).

Lightning normally strikes the tallest object in the area. A building or a vehicle is generally a safe place. Avoid viewpoints, open areas, and isolated tall trees. If you are caught on a trail during a storm, seek a low-lying area for protection. Keep clear of tall objects such as rock formations or lone trees. If there is no place to seek shelter, squat low to the ground, place your hands on your knees with your head between them, making yourself as small as possible. If you are on a lake, head for shore immediately. If you are fishing, a metal or graphite fishing pole can serve as a lightning rod.

Another fact to keep in mind: most lightning deaths occur at the beginning or end of the thunderstorm.

If people are injured by lightning, treat the person who has the most extensive injuries first and call for help. A person struck by lightning carries no electrical charge. A person who appears dead can sometimes be resuscitated by performing CPR.

Along with the thunderstorm, heavy rains are possible in the mountains, with associated flash flooding. These thunderstorms are associated with the monsoon season in Utah, from July to September. This is when the subtropical high becomes established over the southwest part of the country. When the high pressure center is located over southcentral Colorado/northcentral New Mexico, tropical moisture streams northward into Utah. The source region of this moisture is Mexico and the Baja area.

If heavy rains hit, head for higher ground away from rivers, streams, creeks, or normally dry washes. A normally dry streambed can become a raging torrent in just a few minutes. These rains can be highly localized. It need not even be raining in your area for a flash flood to occur. Never try to cross moving and/or rising water because it may be deeper and flowing more rapidly than it appears.

The current weather forecast, along with weather observations, radar data, and much more information, is available on the Internet. Visit the National Weather Service website at http://nimbo.wrh.noaa.gov/saltlake.

Low Impact Hiking and Camping

Utah's mountain environment is rugged, yet fragile. As more people venture outdoors for recreation and relaxation, the mountains will suffer. Trail erosion, garbage, and human waste have become common problems in the mountains and forests of Utah. This spoilage is particularly alarming because the number of people playing outdoors is increasing at an exponential rate.

Recreational use of America's wildlands flourished during the 1960s and 1970s. Although this trend leveled off during the 1980s, it picked up dramatically in the 1990s. The impact from this increased use is quite apparent in many areas of the state. Once-pristine meadows and forests are now eyesores from the scars of campfires, latrines, and garbage. Water, soils, and wildlife habitat have been damaged, as well as opportunities for peace and solitude in a natural setting.

The growing popularity of peak-bagging in Utah could compound the problems if hikers and climbers are not respectful of sensitive ecosystems.

Forester and philosopher Aldo Leopold summed up an ethical approach to nature in *A Sand County Almanac:* "A thing is right when it tends to preserve the integrity, stability and beauty of the biotic community. It is wrong when it tends otherwise."

Early outdoors people, like Leopold, learned long ago the value of preserving the environment. They realized that the outdoors should be left so future visitors can see it in the same condition. The phrase "take only pictures, leave only footprints" grew out of this understanding.

Teaching the "Leave No Trace" concept can be traced back to the 1970s, when outdoor recreation was on the rise. At that time, the National Outdoor Leadership School (NOLS), founded in 1965 by mountaineer Paul Petzoldt, insisted that low impact hiking and camping was the only way to preserve wilderness for future visitors. Since 1991, NOLS has been teaching Leave No Trace as part of a cooperative program with the U.S. Forest Service, the Bureau of Land Management, the National Park Service, and the U.S. Fish and Wildlife Service.

The five principles of Leave No Trace are simple and mostly common sense.
1. Plan ahead and prepare.
- Know the regulations for the area you plan to visit.
- Visit the backcountry in small groups.
- Avoid popular areas during times of high use.
- Choose equipment and clothing in subdued colors, except during hunting season.
- Repackage food into reusable containers.

2. Camp and travel on durable surfaces.
> • Stay on designated trails. Walk single file in the middle of the path.
> • If you must travel off a trail, avoid walking on sensitive vegetation if possible, using rocks and other hard surfaces.
> • Do not shortcut switchbacks.
> • Avoid making cairns or tying ribbons on plants to mark trails.
> • Choose an established campsite that will not be damaged by your stay. Good campsites are found, not made.
> • Restrict activities to the area where vegetation is compacted or absent.
> • Keep pollutants out of water sources by camping at least two hundred feet from lakes and streams.

3. Pack it in, pack it out.
> • Pack everything out that you bring in.
> • Store foods securely and pick up all spilled foods.
> • Deposit human waste in six- to eight-inch-deep holes at least two hundred feet from water sources. Cover the holes and pack out any used toilet paper.
> • Do not wash dishes in streams.
> • Inspect your campsite for trash and any evidence of your stay. Pack out all trash belonging to you and to other people.

4. Leave what you find.
> • Leave plants, rocks, and historical artifacts as you find them.
> • Let nature's sounds prevail. Keep loud voices and noises to a minimum.

5. Minimize the use and impact of fires.
> • Carry a lightweight stove for cooking. Use candles instead of campfires at night.
> • Where fires are permitted, use established fire rings.
> • Do not snap branches off trees, alive or dead.
> • Put out campfires completely.
> • Remove all unburned trash from the fire ring, and scatter the cool ashes over a large area well away from camp.

For more information about Leave No Trace, NOLS has a toll-free telephone line at 1-800-332-4100. Information is also available on the Internet at http://www.lnt.org

Wilderness

The Utah deserts and plateaus and canyons are not a country
of big returns, but a country of spiritual healing, incomparable
for contemplation, meditation, solitude, quiet, awe, peace of
mind and body. We were born of wilderness, and we respond
to it more than we sometimes realize. We depend upon it
increasingly for relief from the termite life we have created.
Factories, power plants, resorts, we can make anywhere.
Wilderness, once we have given it up, is beyond our recon-
struction.

—Wallace Stegner, 1909–1993
From an introduction to *Wilderness at the Edge*, 1992

When newspaper editor Horace Greeley said "go west," Americans did just
that—crossing the North American continent in droves. They ventured into
the wilderness, a place that was wild and free, untouched for the most part by
large populations of people.

Today, wilderness abounds in the West, including Utah. But a growing
population and its demand for limited natural resources are threatening those
wildlands.

In 1964, Congress passed the Wilderness Act and established the National
Wilderness Preservation System. That act defined wilderness as "an area where
the earth and its community of life are untrammeled by man, where man himself is a visitor who does not remain." To qualify for wilderness designation,
areas must offer outstanding opportunities for solitude or a primitive and
unconfined type of recreation, and contain ecological, geological, or other features of scientific, scenic, or historic value. In addition, human influence must
be substantially unnoticeable.

Outside of Alaska, Utah is perhaps the only state with vast amounts of wild
lands that remain in much the same condition as when wagon trains first
moved into the territory.

The Wilderness Act states: "In order to assure that an increasing population, accompanied by expanding settlement and growing mechanization, does
not occupy and modify all areas within the United States and its possessions,
leaving no lands designated for preservation and protection in their natural
condition, it is hereby declared to be the policy of the Congress to secure for
the American people of present and future generations the benefits of an
enduring resource of wilderness."

COUGAR

The act applies only to certain Forest Service, Park Service, and Fish and Wildlife Service lands.

In 1976, Congress enacted the Federal Lands Policy Management Act, requiring the Bureau of Land Management to take an inventory of its holdings to see which lands were suitable for wilderness designation. The number of BLM acres that should be set aside as wilderness was a hotly debated topic at the time when this book was written.

Many of Utah's county high peaks are in or near wilderness areas and BLM wilderness study areas. Various restrictions may apply to hiking and camping in these areas. The regulations are likely more strict than those in the national forests. Check with local Forest Service or BLM offices before venturing into these preservation areas.

County High Peaks

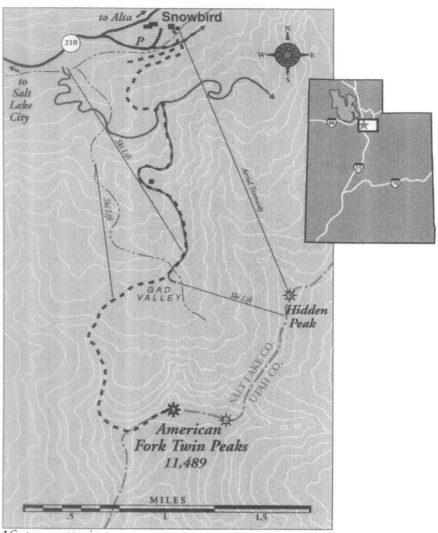

N
W — *E*
S

to Alta ↗ **Snowbird**

P

(210)

to
Salt
Lake
City

Ski Lift

Ski Lift

Aerial Thramvay

*GAD
VALLEY*

Ski Lift

☀
*Hidden
Peak*

SALT LAKE CO.
UTAH CO.

☀   ☀
*American
Fork Twin Peaks
11,489*

MILES
.5   1   1.5

* *Contours are approximate*

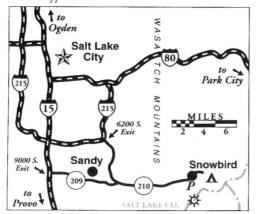

↑ to
Ogden

**Salt Lake
City** ☆

W
A
S
A
T
C
H

(215)

(80)

to
Park City

(15)
(215)

M
O
U
N
T
A
I
N
S

*6200 S.
Exit*

MILES
2   4   6

*9000 S.
Exit* ↙

Sandy
●

Snowbird
Δ

(209)   (210)
P

to
Provo ↓

☀

SALT LAKE CO.

– – – – Route
━━(235)━━ Secondary Road
░░░░░░░░ Dirt Road
⋯⋯⋯⋯ 4WD Road
━[89]━ US Highway
━[15]━ Interstate
—–—–— Stream
Δ Campground
☀ Summit
P Parking

12

American Fork Twin Peaks
11,489 feet
Salt Lake County

Time:  6–7 hours   3–4.5 hours

Distance: 8 miles

Difficulty: Difficult

Starting Elevation: 8,040 feet

Elevation Gain: 3,449 feet

USGS Map: Dromedary Peak

➤ Trailhead

• From Interstate 215 (on the east side of the valley) in Salt Lake City, take Exit 6200 South, and head south on Utah Highway 210. This highway will turn east as it climbs into Little Cottonwood Canyon.

• Park in the Entry 2 lot at Snowbird Ski and Summer Resort and follow the signs to Snowbird Center.

➤ Camping

Tanner Flat and Albion Basin campgrounds are located farther up Little Cottonwood Canyon from Snowbird. Both charge fees and have water and restroom facilities.

➤ Tips and Precautions

Be on the lookout for unexploded shells used for avalanche control during the winter. Also, don't be lured into an "easy" climb by taking the tram to the top of nearby Hidden Peak. The knife-edge traverse from Hidden Peak to American Fork Twin is trickier than the route from the western side of the resort.

THE NORTH FACE

13

THE VIEW WEST TO THE PFEIFFERHORN

➤ The Hike

From the east end of the parking lot, walk across the bridge to a dirt road that continues east. Just past the footbridge on the left, coming from the Snowbird Center, catch the beginning of the trail on the right. The trail is well marked and runs along Dick Bass Highway, named after the resort's owner and first person ever to climb the highest peak on each of the seven continents. The trail climbs under Wilbre ski lift. At a junction, the route cuts back to the left along a dirt road, which leads to the top of Wilbre ski lift. Follow the road that branches off, uphill, to the right.

This road climbs past Mid-Gad Restaurant, but don't expect to pick up a sandwich here. The restaurant is closed during the summer.

Near the base of Little Cloud ski lift, the marked trail continues up toward Hidden Peak, but the best route to American Fork Twin Peaks veers to the right, up a ski run called Election, which starts up a steep, open slope. This run, which is a broad clearing during the summer, is a climbing traverse to the top of Gad 2 ski lift. From here, you'll have a spectacular view of Gad Valley and the higher of the twin peaks towering over it.

Continue southwest, away from the ski area, and climb a steep talus slope to a minor saddle along the top of the ridge. This short climb is probably the most difficult section of the hike. Not only is it steep, hikers must be wary of unexploded missiles. These devices are used during the winter to trigger avalanches, and this particular hillside is covered with debris from exploded shells. Signs throughout Snowbird warn about the danger of running across one that hasn't blown up . . . yet.

14

Once on the ridge, follow it to the top of a peak just west of Salt Lake County's highest summit. At times, the ridge narrows to a knife edge and winds can be particularly tricky. From the top of this peak, you get a good view of both twins. The route continues along the ridge, dropping down to a saddle before climbing up the west summit, which is the higher of the twins. The perilous cliffs of the north face drop 1,400 feet to Gad Valley below. From the summit, you can look down upon the ski resort and Little Cottonwood Canyon, as well as the Pfeifferhorn (Little

HIKERS CLIMB ALONG THE RIDGE

Matterhorn) to the west. You can also see Mount Timpanogos, one of our Utah Classic hikes, to the south and the Uinta Mountains in the east. The return trip is along the same route.

➤ Background

During summer months, the ski runs at Snowbird are used by hikers—some serious, others just out for a Sunday stroll in the mountains. Most of the resort is on Forest Service land in the Wasatch National Forest. The resort has identified and marked one specific trail that takes hikers from Snowbird Center, the base of the aerial tram, to the top of the resort on 10,992-foot Hidden Peak.

The Twin Peaks rise nearly 500 feet higher. The higher of the twins is the western peak, 11,489 feet. Its shorter, eastern sister stands 11,433 feet tall.

➤ For More Information
  • Wasatch-Cache National Forest, Salt Lake Ranger District, 6944 S. 3000 East, Salt Lake City, UT 84121, (801) 943-1794.
  • *Hiking the Wasatch*, by John Veranth, Wasatch Mountain Club, 1988.

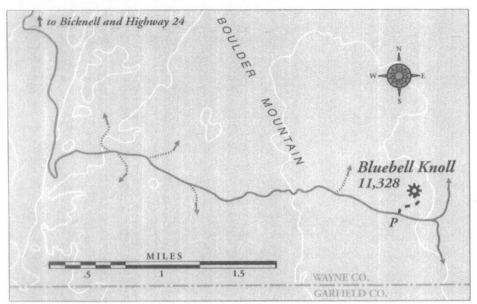

to Bicknell and Highway 24

BOULDER MOUNTAIN

**Bluebell Knoll
11,328**

P

MILES

.5   1   1.5

WAYNE CO.

GARFIELD CO.

* *Contours are approximate*

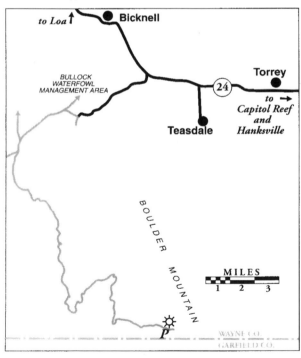

to Loa↑

Bicknell

BULLOCK
WATERFOWL
MANAGEMENT AREA

Torrey

24

to
Capitol Reef
and
Hanksville

Teasdale

B O U L D E R   M O U N T A I N

MILES

1   2   3

WAYNE CO.

GARFIELD CO.

P

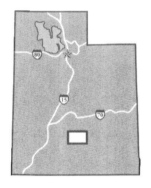

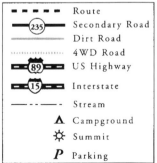

Route

235   Secondary Road

Dirt Road

4WD Road

89   US Highway

15   Interstate

Stream

▲   Campground

☼   Summit

P   Parking

Bluebell Knoll
11,328 feet*
Wayne County

Time:  10 minutes

Distance: 0.5 miles

Difficulty: Easy

Starting Elevation: 11,208 feet

Elevation Gain: 120 feet

USGS Maps: Government Point and Blind Lake

➤ Trailhead
• Drive east on Utah Highway 24 from the east end of Bicknell.
• After 2.5 miles, turn right/south on a paved road.
• Drive 3.8 miles to a junction. A sign offers directions to Kings Ranch and Boulder Top. Take a right on the dirt road to Boulder Top.
• After 3.6 miles, the road splits. Take the left fork.
• 0.7 mile farther, catch Forest Service Road 178.
• Drive 12.8 miles to a gate, which is open to vehicles from June 16 to October 31. From here, the road climbs up onto the Aquarius Plateau.
• Stay on the main road for 3.2 miles. A sign along the road designates Bluebell Knoll.

➤ Camping
From the looks of it, there are numerous places to camp on the plateau itself, but any facilities may be miles away. There's a BLM campground, Sunglow, just south of Bicknell.

➤ Tips and Precautions
It could be easy to get lost on the plateau looking for the highest point. You should carry a detailed map and compass to help find Bluebell Knoll.

*The USGS 1:100,000 map shows the elevation of Bluebell Knoll as 11,328 feet, but a sign at its base says 11,322 feet.

PHOTO BY MICHAEL R. WEIBEL

17

THE TOP OF BOULDER MOUNTAIN

► The Hike

Getting to the trailhead, if that's what you want to call it, is really more of an adventure than the hike itself. From the Bluebell Knoll sign, the hike to the top of the hill takes only a matter of minutes. Look for the biggest boulder and climb on top of it. The surrounding plateau is quite inviting.

► Background

The Aquarius Plateau is an area about 35 miles long and 15 miles wide, parts of which have been called Boulder Mountain, Boulder Top, and Escalante Mountain. It is located in the Dixie National Forest.

In his book *Utah Place Names*, John W. Van Cott said the plateau was named in the mid-1870s by A. H. Thompson of the Powell Surveys. He was reportedly the first white person to cross the plateau. According to Van Cott, the Aquarius is perhaps the grandest of all Utah's high plateaus. He said it is best described by some of the explorers, geologists, and surveyors who worked their way across it.

"The slopes we were crossing were full of leaping torrents and clear lakes," wrote Frederick Dellenbaugh.* "They were so covered with these that the plateau afterwards was given the name Aquarius."

*In *A Canyon Voyage: The Narrative of the Second Powell Expedition down the Green-Colorado River from Wyoming and the Explorations on Land in the Years 1871 and 1872* (Putnam, 1908).

RAFT LAKE FROM BLUEBELL KNOLL

Today, the names of landmarks on the plateau give a good idea of the Aquarius: Riddle Flat, Lightning Flat, Donkey Meadows, Grass Lake, Stink Flats, Little Beef Meadows, and Lake in the Flat Meadows.

Clarence Edward Dutton said the plateau's "broad summit is clad with dense forests of spruces opening in grassy parks, and sprinkled with scores of lakes filled by the melting snows. We have seen it afar off, its long straight crest-line stretched across the sky like the threshold of another world. On three sides, south, west and east, it is walled by dark battlements of volcanic rock, and its long slopes beneath descend into the dismal desert. The explorer who sits upon the brink of its parapet looking off into the southern and eastern haze, who skirts its lava-cap or clambers up and down its vast ravines, who builds his campfire by the borders of its snow-fed lakes or stretches himself beneath its giant pines and spruces, forgets that he is a geologist and feels himself a poet." His comments were written in 1872 for John Wesley Powell's *Geology of the High Plateaus of Utah* (1880).

➤ For More Information
• Dixie National Forest, Teasdale Ranger District, 138 E. Main St., Teasdale, UT 84773, (435) 425-3702.

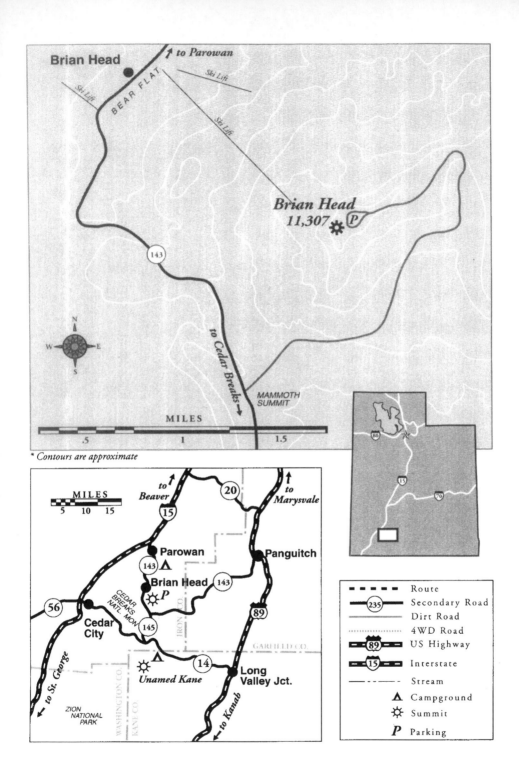

Brian Head

to Parowan

BEAR FLAT

Ski Lift

Ski Lift

Ski Lift

143

Brian Head
11,307

P

N
W   E
S

to Cedar Breaks

MAMMOTH
SUMMIT

MILES

.5   1   1.5

* Contours are approximate

MILES
5   10   15

to
Beaver

20

to
Marysvale

15

Parowan

Panguitch

143

Brian Head

143

CEDAR BREAKS NATL. MON.

P

89

56

Cedar
City

145

IRON CO.

GARFIELD CO.

14

to St. George

Unamed Kane

Long
Valley Jct.

ZION
NATIONAL
PARK

WASHINGTON CO.

KANE CO.

to Kanab

80

13

70

Route

235   Secondary Road

Dirt Road

4WD Road

89   US Highway

15   Interstate

Stream

Campground

Summit

P   Parking

20

Brian Head

11,307 feet
Iron County

Time: —
Distance: —
Difficulty: Too Easy
Starting Elevation: 11,307 feet
Elevation Gain: —
USGS Map: Brian Head

➤ Trailhead
• Take the Parowan exit from Interstate 15, turning onto Utah Highway 143. The road climbs through the colorful Hurricane Cliffs.
• After passing through the resort community of Brian Head, continue driving to a point just beyond mile marker 17, where a gravel road heads left/east and is marked by the Brian Head Peak and Vista Peak sign.
• Drive 3 miles to the summit.

➤ Camping
There's a campground, Vermillion Castle, just beyond mile marker 6 as you drive from Parowan to Brian Head. There is a fee, and the campground includes water and restroom facilities.

➤ Tips and Precautions
Needless to say, this isn't much of a hike considering the fact that you can drive right up to the summit. Don't expect privacy. Brian Head is a resort community with a variety of activities going on throughout the year. You might opt to leave your car at the bottom of the ski slopes and ride a mountain bike to the summit. Or simply take off on a hike around the summit or along the resort's ski trails.

THE DIRT ROAD LEADS TO THE TOP OF BRIAN HEAD

21

THE SUMMIT SHELTER WAS BUILT IN 1935 BY THE CIVILIAN CONSERVATION CORPS

➤ The Hike

Because this is a drive and not a hike to the summit, make it a hike anyway. Park at the bottom of the road that climbs up to the summit and walk.

➤ Background

A nice rock shelter marks the summit of Brian Head Peak, which overlooks the ski resort and town of the same name. The town, by the way, is the highest town in Utah. The shelter was built in 1935 by the Civilian Conservation Corps. It was renovated in 1995 by Sierra Club members on a southwest service trip.

Brian Head was originally called Monument Peak; according to one story, its name was changed to honor William Jennings Bryan, a former presidential candidate and lawyer in the famous Scopes monkey trial. If "The Great Commoner" hadn't lost that landmark case dealing with evolution to Clarence Darrow, the peak's name might have kept the same spelling. For some unknown reason, the spelling was changed when the moniker was made official.

Brian Head Peak sits atop the Markagunt Plateau. According to John Van Cott's *Utah Place Names*, the plateau was named after a Piute Indian word meaning "highland of trees." It was named by Almon Thompson, a member of John Wesley Powell's survey team.

BRIAN HEAD

The summit provides a spectacular view of the giant 2,500-foot-high natural amphitheater at Cedar Breaks National Monument. On a clear day, you can see into parts of Nevada and Arizona.

➤ For More Information
• Dixie National Forest, Cedar City Ranger District, 82 N. 100 East, Cedar City, UT 84720, (435) 865-3200.

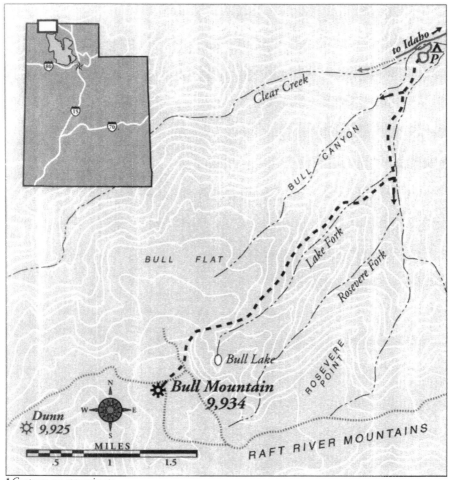

* Contours are approximate

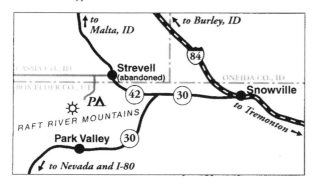

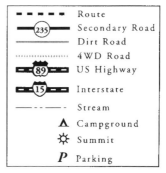

Bull Mountain
9,934 feet
Box Elder County

Time: 🐢 7–8 hours   🐇 4–5.5 hours
Distance: 9 miles
Difficulty: Moderate
Starting Elevation: 6,320 feet
Elevation Gain: 3,614 feet
USGS Maps: Rosevere Point and Standrod

➤ Trailhead
• Take the second (north) Snowville/Park Valley exit from Interstate 84, turning left/west onto Utah Highway 30/42.
• Drive 24 miles northwest, passing the junction where Utah Highway 30 turns left/south. Continue on Utah Highway 42, heading northwest.
• Shortly after crossing into Idaho, turn left/west onto a dirt road. This is after passing some abandoned homes in Strevell.
• Drive 3 miles and take a left/south on a road that leads into Clear Creek Canyon. This road will eventually bend around to the west and into the drainage.
• After approximately 5 miles, you'll cross Clear Creek. Continue for another 0.75 mile to Clear Creek Campground. Turn left across the stream and into the campground.
• The trailhead begins where the road loops at the end of the campground.

➤ Camping
    Clear Creek Campground has water and restrooms, with a couple of sites right at the trailhead.

➤ Tips and Precautions
    The trail becomes faint and difficult to follow on the upper section of Lake Fork Canyon. Getting caught in old deadfall can make it a bit frustrating. If necessary, climb up along the right/west slope and work your way up canyon through the sagebrush.
    The summit is atop a long, flat plateau. A map, compass, and altimeter will help locate Box Elder County's highest peak.

THE NORTH FACE OF THE BULL MOUNTAIN PLATEAU

➤ The Hike

From the trailhead, hike south along an old 4-wheel-drive road that is used mostly by ATVs. The trail climbs gently toward the Raft River Mountains. In less than a mile, the road reaches a junction with another road heading right/west to Bull Flat. Stay left and continue south until reaching the Lake Creek junction.

Turn right here and start climbing southwest along Lake Fork. After a short while, the trail narrows to a single track as it climbs the drainage on the left side of the stream. After the trail crosses the stream, it will become more narrow and less distinct. Try to follow the trail as it parallels the creek to the marsh below Bull Lake. If you lose the trail, just veer up to the right until you reach a clearing above the trees and below the cliffs.

From the Bull Lake marsh, an obvious trail starts on the right/north and climbs along and above the cliffs. The summit is a small pile of rocks on the flat plateau about half a mile west-southwest of the cliffs overlooking Bull Lake.

➤ Background

Bull Mountain is in the Raft River Mountains, a small east-west range along the northernmost point in Box Elder County. The range was named after nearby Raft River, which early settlers crossed on primitive rafts.

The summit is not named on maps. Roads, used primarily by ranchers in the area, crisscross the summit plateau. One of these roads leads from the summit to nearby Dunn peak, 9,925 feet, which reportedly has a building on it and has been assumed by some people to be the county's highest peak.

Dunn is surrounded by a 9,920-foot contour line on maps. Bull Mountain

MIKE POSTHOLES UP THE MOUNTAIN AFTER A LATE SPRING SNOWSTORM

is also surrounded by a 9,920-foot contour line, but altimeter measurements conclude that Bull is the higher of the two peaks.

➤ For More Information
  • Sawtooth National Forest, Burley Ranger District, 2621 S. Overland Ave., Burley, ID 83318, (208) 678-0430.

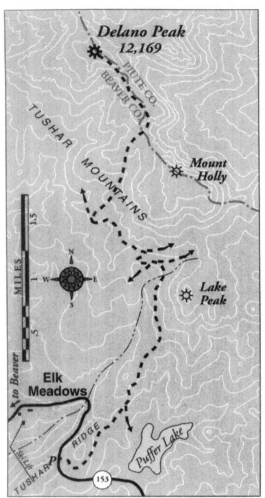

Delano Peak
12,169

PIUTE CO.
BEAVER CO.

TUSHAR

MOUNTAINS

Mount
Holly

Lake
Peak

MILES

1.5

.5

to Beaver

Elk
Meadows

TUSHAR

RIDGE

Ski Lift

P

Puffer Lake

153

* Contours are approximate

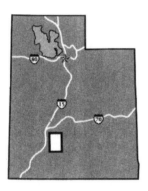

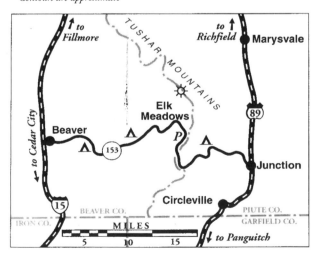

to
Fillmore

TUSHAR   MOUNTAINS

to
Richfield   Marysvale

to Cedar City

Beaver

153

Elk
Meadows

P

89

Junction

Circleville

15

BEAVER CO.

PIUTE CO.

IRON CO.

GARFIELD CO.

MILES

5   10   15

to Panguitch

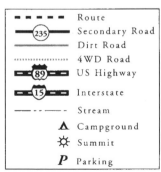

━ ━ ━ ━   Route
━(235)━   Secondary Road
━━━━━   Dirt Road
·········   4WD Road
━(89)━   US Highway
━(15)━   Interstate
─·─·─   Stream
▲   Campground
☼   Summit
P   Parking

28

Delano Peak
12,169 feet*
Beaver and Piute Counties

Time:  5–6 hours   3–3.75 hours

Distance: 10 miles

Difficulty: Moderate

Starting Elevation: 10,040 feet

Elevation Gain: 2,129 feet

USGS Maps: Delano Peak and Shelly Baldy Peak

➤ Trailhead

• Take the Beaver exit from Interstate 15, turning east on Utah Highway 153.
• Elk Meadows Ski and Summer Resort is about 18 miles from Beaver.
Continue past the resort, where the road turns back on itself.
• Before reaching Puffer Lake, 0.5 mile beyond mile marker 20, the Forest
Service trail begins on the left/north side of the highway. This is a poorly
marked trailhead, so keep an eye open for the small Forest Service trail/road
marker off the side of the highway.

➤ Camping

Mahogany Cove Campground is just beyond mile marker 11 on Utah
Highway 153, between Beaver and Elk Meadows. It has drinking water and
restroom facilities. There is a fee.

➤ Tips and Precautions

There is no trail on the upper part of this hike,
which climbs above timberline. Landmarks, such as
peaks and drainages, are easy to spot.

Shortly after you leave the trailhead, your trail is
joined on the right by a trail from Puffer Lake. Pay
close attention on the return trip so you don't wander down the wrong trail. The Puffer Lake trail is
more distinct to people hiking downhill.

*USGS maps say Delano Peak is 12,169 feet above sea level,
while a sign on the summit records its elevation as 12,173 feet.

THE SUMMIT SIGN

29

THE SOUTH FACE OF DELANO. THE ROUTE FOLLOWS THE RIGHT SHOULDER.

➤ The Hike

From the highway, a trail scrambles for a few feet and veers right. Follow this trail/road for another 125 to 150 feet, to a point where it meets a marked trail on the left/northeast.

The left trail gently climbs into the forest. In a short distance, the trail is joined by one coming from Puffer Lake on the right/southeast. Continue on the same trail, which is occasionally obscured by fallen timber.

Shortly after you emerge from the trees at a stream crossing, you will see the trail marked as Forest Service 175. Continue a short way until your trail intersects with the Skyline National Recreation Trail. A trail sign points back to Puffer Lake on 175, and to Big Flat and Big Johns Flat along the Skyline Trail.

Turn left/west on the Skyline Trail and follow it as it wraps around the base of Mount Holly, 11,985 feet. Follow the trail until it crosses two bridges. After the second bridge, venture off the trail to the right/northeast and climb a drainage to the saddle between Holly and Delano. The route from here to the top is above timberline and covered with grasses and wildflowers.

As you approach the top of the drainage, it widens and you will get your first glimpse of the main portion of Delano. The ridge from Holly runs northwest and separates Beaver and Piute counties. The trail running up the side of the mountain may appear steep and menacing, but it is relatively safe. You should be careful, however, of the loose scree.

A sign and register mark the summit, which provides a captivating view of Belknap and the old mining roads on its flanks. Lucky hikers will see the small herd of mountain goats that live around Holly and Delano.

➤ Background

Few people realize that Utah has spectacular 12,000-foot peaks outside of the Uinta Mountains. The volcanic Tushar Mountains, for example, are home to Delano Peak, the highest mountain in Beaver and Piute counties as well as all of central Utah.

Delano was named for Secretary of the Interior Columbus Delano, who served under President Grant. The lofty peak is not as popular with photographers as nearby Mount Belknap and Mount Baldy, to the north, which are bare, rocky domes jutting out of the forest. But that's not to say Delano is not a fine hike. M. Biddle, author of *Fishlake National Forest Backcountry Guide for Hiking and Horseback Riding*, said it could be the easiest 12,000-foot mountain to climb in the West.

THE LAST STEEP SHOULDER OF DELANO

➤ For More Information
• Fishlake National Forest, Beaver Ranger District, 575 S. Main St., Beaver, UT 84713, (435) 438-2436.
• *Fishlake National Forest Backcountry Guide for Hiking and Horseback Riding*, by M. Biddle, Wasatch, 1993.

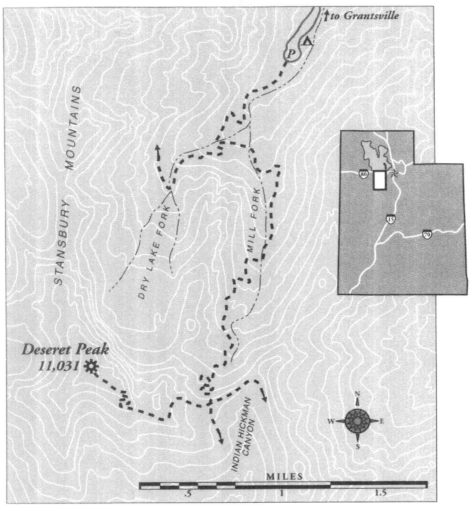

Deseret Peak
11,031

DRY LAKE FORK

MILL FORK

INDIAN HICKMAN CANYON

STANSBURY MOUNTAINS

to Grantsville

* Contours are approximate

MILES

.5   1   1.5

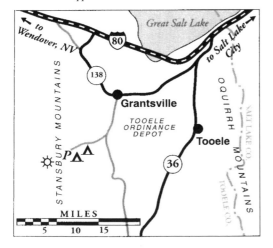

to Wendover, NV

Great Salt Lake

to Salt Lake City

Grantsville

TOOELE ORDINANCE DEPOT

Tooele

STANSBURY MOUNTAINS

OQUIRRH MOUNTAINS

SALT LAKE CO.

TOOELE CO.

MILES

5   10   15

▪ ▪ ▪ ▪ ▪	Route
235	Secondary Road
	Dirt Road
···········	4WD Road
89	US Highway
15	Interstate
– · – · –	Stream
▲	Campground
☼	Summit
P	Parking

Deseret Peak

11,031 feet
Tooele County

Time: 5.25–6 hours  2.25–3.75 hours

Distance: 6.5 miles

Difficulty: Moderate

Starting Elevation: 7,418 feet

Elevation Gain: 3,613 feet

USGS Maps: Deseret Peak East and Deseret Peak West

➤ Trailhead
• Drive west on Interstate 80 from Salt Lake City.
• Take the Grantsville/Tooele exit, Exit 99. Drive 3.5 miles to the junction of Utah Highway 138. Turn right/west and head toward Grantsville.
• Drive 11.2 miles into Grantsville. A sign points to Wasatch National Forest recreation sites. Take a left/south.
• Drive 5.1 miles to a junction. Take a right/west, leading to South Willow Canyon.
• The pavement ends after a little more than 3 miles, at the national forest boundary.
• The trailhead is another 4 miles up the road, at the end of Loop Campground.

➤ Camping
There are four campgrounds along the road in South Willow Canyon.

➤ Tips and Precautions
Immediately after the stream crossing, the route cuts sharply back to the left and follows alongside the stream. Because of bank erosion, the trail is not readily noticeable. Then, about 50 feet from the crossing, it forks. Be sure to take the left fork.

NORTH COULOIR

33

DIANE BUSH ON A LATE SUMMER SNOWFIELD BEFORE THE LAST PUSH TO THE SUMMIT

➤ The Hike

From the trailhead, which can be quite crowded during the summer, the trail climbs south at a moderate grade as it meanders through a lush aspen forest. After roughly 0.75 mile, it crosses a large stream. Although early in the hike, this is a critical juncture because it's easy to miss the trail after crossing the water. The trail cuts back to the left/east along the stream bank. Then, just a few steps down the trail as it wanders back into the trees, it forks. Take the left/east trail to Mill Fork.

The well-trodden trail climbs 1,800 feet in 1.5 miles as it winds up and through grassy meadows filled with an abundance of wildflowers. Where the trees thin near the head of the canyon, the trail starts to switchback up a cirque that forms a natural amphitheater. From this point, you can look back and catch glimpses of the Salt Lake Valley, including Stansbury Island.

At the saddle, the route turns right and heads up a ridge. A sign should point to the peak. There may be patches of snow along this ridge until early summer. The summit is a relatively easy hike from here. On a clear day atop the peak, you can see as far north as the Wellsville Mountains, southeast to Mount Nebo, and southwest to Ibapah Peak.

➤ Background

Deseret Peak is the highest point in the Stansbury Mountains, west of Salt Lake City. The range was named after Capt. Howard Stansbury, who surveyed the Great Salt Lake in 1850. Deseret was the name of the Mormon state that

DIANE BUSH CLIMBS A STEEP SNOW FIELD JUST ABOVE THE SADDLE

AFTER CLIMBING OUT OF THE LOWER FOREST, THE NORTH PEAKS POP INTO VIEW

preceded Utah. It is a *Book of Mormon* term meaning honeybee—a reference to Mormon industriousness.

Historian Jay Haymon, according to a series of stories in *The Salt Lake Tribune*, said the peak was likely named by a Mormon pioneer. "The pioneers were probably working and using the land and they probably called it Deseret for industry because of that hard work," he said.

Today, the Stansbury Mountains are popular for outdoor recreation. In 1984, Congress helped preserve the 25,500 acres around Deseret Peak by establishing the Deseret Peak Wilderness.

➤ For More Information
  • Wasatch-Cache National Forest, Salt Lake Ranger District, 6944 S. 3000 East, Salt Lake City, UT 84121, (801) 524-5042.
  • *Hiking Utah*, by Dave Hall, Falcon Press, 1997.

Photo by Diane Bush

MIKE AND DAN CLOWN AROUND ON THE SUMMIT

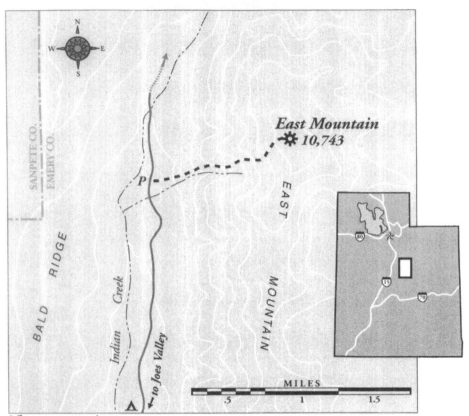

East Mountain
☼ *10,743*

EAST MOUNTAIN

BALD RIDGE

Indian Creek

to Joes Valley

P

SANPETE CO.
EMERY CO.

* *Contours are approximate*

MILES
.5   1   1.5

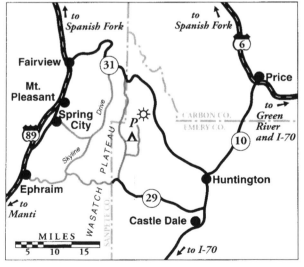

to
Spanish Fork

to
Spanish Fork

Fairview

Mt.
Pleasant

Spring
City

Ephraim

to
Manti

Price

to
Green
River
and I-70

Huntington

Castle Dale

to I-70

CARBON CO.
EMERY CO.

WASATCH PLATEAU

SANPETE CO.

Drive

Skyline

MILES
5   10   15

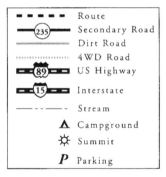

	Route
235	Secondary Road
	Dirt Road
	4WD Road
89	US Highway
15	Interstate
	Stream
▲	Campground
☼	Summit
P	Parking

East Mountain*
10,743 feet
Emery County

Time: 🐢 2–3.5 hours 🐇 1–1.5 hours

Distance: 2 miles

Difficulty: Moderate

Starting Elevation: 9,120 feet

Elevation Gain: 1,623 feet

USGS Map: Rilda Canyon

➤ Trailhead
• From Castle Dale, drive west on Utah Highway 29.
• At the north end of Joes Valley Reservoir, turn right on Upper Joes Valley Road.
• After 1.1 miles, the road forks. Veer to the right, which goes to Upper Joes Valley.
• It forks again in another 1.1 miles. Stay on the right.
• Drive 5.7 miles. Turn right/east.
• After 0.7 mile, turn left/north, following signs to Indian Creek Campground.
• The campground is 1.3 miles down this road. Continue past the campground for 2.1 miles, on what is called Spoon Creek Road. Park near the cattle guard.

(A quicker approach from many Utah cities starts at Fairview. Take Utah Highway 31 east for 18 miles, then go right/south for 13 miles on a dirt road that leads to Joes Valley Reservoir. Turn left/east and follow signs to Indian Creek Campground.)

➤ Camping
Indian Creek Campground has water and restroom facilities. There is a fee, and reservations are required.

➤ Tips and Precautions
This is one of the few Utah county high peaks that has no trail at all. Stay on the left side of the drainage and look for deer trails.

The roads leading to East Mountain can become slick and treacherous with a little bit of rainfall. Keep updated about weather conditions.

*See the background information about Monument Peak (page 69), showing how hikes for East Mountain, Monument Peak, and South Tent Mountain can be combined into one trip.

MIKE BUSHWHACKS THROUGH THE BRUSH ON EAST MOUNTAIN

THE SUMMIT OF EAST MOUNTAIN

➤ The Hike

From the trailhead, East Mountain climbs above a lush forest that must be negotiated because there is no trail.

To reach the highest point in Emery County, start on the left/north side of the fence and follow it east from the cattle guard in the road. Stay on the north side of this fence and expect to cross some deadfall. Continue hiking east along the left/north side of a drainage. Aim for a steep clearing below the summit. The grass can grow quite tall, making it difficult to negotiate steps as the route climbs up the hillside. In the clearing, you'll cross what's left of a road that was built to maintain a water line leading to a mine.

The summit is atop a large rock slab.

➤ Background

East Mountain has the steepest overall grade of any of Utah's county high peaks. Although it's only a 2-mile round-trip hike, the route gains 1,623 feet in 1 mile.

➤ For More Information

• Manti-La Sal National Forest, Ferron Ranger District, 98 S. State St., Ferron, UT 84523, (435) 384-2372.

41

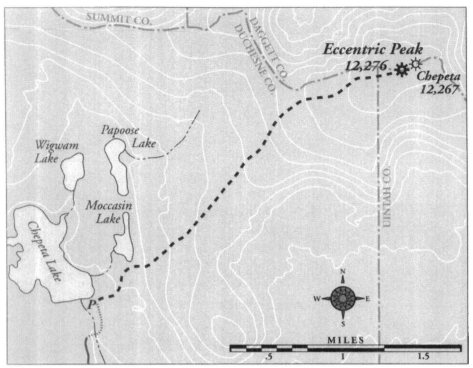

Eccentric Peak
12,276

Chepeta
12,267

Wigwam Lake

Papoose Lake

Moccasin Lake

Chepeta Lake

SUMMIT CO.

DAGGETT CO.

DUCHESNE CO.

UINTAH CO.

P

N
W E
S

MILES
.5   1   1.5

* Contours are approximate

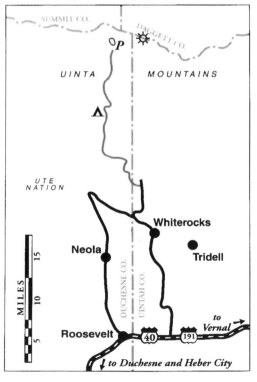

SUMMIT CO.

DAGGETT CO.

P

UINTA   MOUNTAINS

Δ

UTE NATION

DUCHESNE CO.

UINTAH CO.

Whiterocks

Neola

Tridell

MILES
15
10
5

to Vernal

Roosevelt   40   191

to Duchesne and Heber City

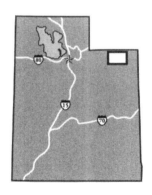

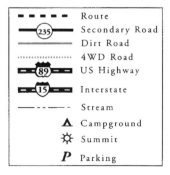

	Route
235	Secondary Road
	Dirt Road
	4WD Road
89	US Highway
15	Interstate
	Stream
Δ	Campground
☼	Summit
P	Parking

Eccentric Peak

12,276 feet
Daggett and Uintah Counties

Time:  2.75–3.5 hours   1.5–2 hours

Distance: 5 miles

Difficulty: Moderate

Starting Elevation: 10,520 feet

Elevation Gain: 1,756 feet

USGS Maps: Whiterocks Lake, and Chepeta Lake

➤ Trailhead
• From the intersection of Utah Highway 121 and U.S. Highway 40/191 in Roosevelt, drive east on U.S. 40/191 for five miles. Just beyond W. Russell Todd School on the left/north, near mile marker 121, turn left/north onto 5750 East (county route 2752).
• Drive north for 20.9 miles. Turn left where the pavement ends and follow signs for Elkhorn Loop Road and Chepeta Lake.
• Continue for 14.5 miles. At the Y intersection, veer right, following the sign to Chepeta Lake.
• Drive 3.7 miles to another junction. Turn right.
• The road crosses a stream after approximately 7 miles. Some people may want to park here and walk the additional quarter-mile to a parking area near the lake.

➤ Camping
   Pole Creek Lake Campground is located near the Y intersection, 14.5 miles after you turn onto the Elkhorn Loop Road. There is a fee, and it has drinking water and restroom facilities.

➤ Tips and Precautions
   This is one of the few Utah county high peak hikes that has no trail from start to finish. A map and compass are essential. Be careful on the talus slope.

SUMMIT SHELTER

43

MIKE DESCENDS THE STEEP TALUS SLOPE

MOCCASIN LAKE BELOW THE TALUS SLOPE LEADING TO THE PLATEAU

➤ The Hike

From the parking area, head northeast across the rolling landscape through a fairly dense forest. In a short distance, the forest ends at the foot of a steep talus slope.

This is perhaps the most difficult part of the hike. Find a safe route up the talus, continuing in a northeast direction. The top of the slope opens into a high Alpine meadow. Once in the meadow, point yourself northeast and walk to the peak. The trek is just less than two miles and climbs gently across the meadows and Mars-like boulder fields to the summit. Rock shelters mark the relatively flat Eccentric Peak and nearby Chepeta Peak, 12,267 feet.

➤ Background

At 10,600 feet, Chepeta Lake is the site of one of the highest trailheads in the Uintas. It is also one of several trailheads along the Highline Trail, which crisscrosses Utah's highest mountain range. This trailhead marks the first point where the Highline Trail touches a road since leaving the Mirror Lake Highway, more than 60 miles away.

➤ For More Information

• Ashley National Forest, Roosevelt Ranger District, 244 W. Highway 40, Roosevelt, UT 84066, (435) 722-5018.

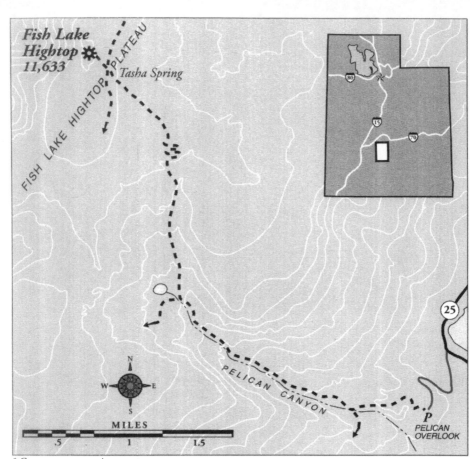

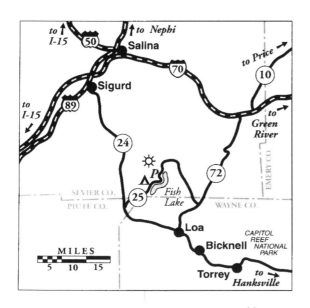

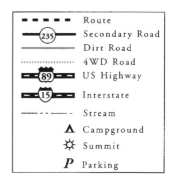

* Contours are approximate

Fish Lake Hightop
11,633 feet
Sevier County

Time:  4.75–5 hours   2.5–3 hours

Distance: 8.5 miles

Difficulty: Moderate

Starting Elevation: 9,150 feet

Elevation Gain: 2,503 feet

USGS Map: Fishlake

➤ Trailhead
• From the north, take Interstate 15 south to Scipio.
• Take Utah Highway 50 south from Scipio to Salina.
• Take U.S. Highway 89 south to Sigurd.
• From there, take Utah Highway 24 south to Utah Highway 25, about 12 miles northwest of Loa.
• Drive northeast on Utah 25 until you reach Fish Lake. The road travels along the northwest side of the lake. The turnoff to the trailhead at Pelican Overlook is near the north side of the lake, on the left side of the road. Follow the gravel road about a mile to the trailhead.

➤ Camping
There are numerous campgrounds around the lake, but most cater to recreational vehicle travelers. Tents are allowed at the Bowery, Doctor Creek, Mackinaw, and Frying Pan campgrounds on the northwest side of the lake. They have drinking water and restroom facilities, and a fee is charged for camping.

➤ Tips and Precautions
Beware of the mosquitoes! DEET or other kinds of repellent may be necessary. Also, there are numerous trails, and animal paths crisscrossing the plateau. Pay attention on the ascent to ensure that the right route is taken for the descent.

JUNCTION SIGN CAN BE MISLEADING

47

MIKE WORKS HIS WAY THROUGH THE LAST SET OF BOULDERS TO THE SUMMIT

➤ The Hike

Shortly after leaving the trailhead, the trail splits. Take the left fork. From here, the trail climbs into Pelican Canyon; at one point, it tunnels through the canopy of an aspen forest.

After approximately 2 miles and 1,300 feet of elevation gain, the trail reaches a junction at the bottom of a meadow. The sign, in 1997, gave two different directions to Fish Lake Hightop. The trail to the left lists a shorter distance, but in reality it is a much longer route to the summit. The sign refers to the distance to the top of the plateau, not to the summit. Take the right trail, which may be difficult to see as it crosses the meadow. Look for cairns. The trail passes by the right side of a small pond, but that is not easy to see on the uphill trip. Eventually the trail switchbacks up a false summit, which actually brings hikers to the top of the plateau. It's not the summit, but the steep part of the hike is over.

The trail vanishes in spots and gets jumbled among a maze of old roads and animal paths on top of the plateau. Keep a close eye out for cairns. Continue northwest to the highest point on the plateau. The summit consists of a heap of large boulders. Scramble to the top of these boulders to find a survey marker designating the top.

➤ Background

The trailhead at Pelican Promontory overlooks one of the state's largest natural freshwater lakes, Fish Lake. It is the namesake for Sevier County's highest point, the mountain range and the national forest that surrounds it. The lake was formed between two parallel faults and was named for the abundance of fish that fed Native Americans who once lived along its shores.

President McKinley reserved the first part of the Fishlake National Forest in 1899 to protect the watershed of Fish Lake and the nearby Fremont River. Overgrazing was damaging the watersheds and causing flash floods that inundated towns and silted irrigation facilities necessary for farming.

More recently, recreation has become popular on and around Fish Lake. According to Forest Service publications, the Fish Lake–Johnson Valley area receives 25 percent of the recreation use on the 1.4-million-acre forest. The area includes 2,500 acres of lake and 670 acres of reservoir. Large mackinaw trout attract anglers to the lake, which can be quite crowded on weekends and holidays.

➤ For More Information
• Fishlake National Forest, Loa Ranger District, 138 S. Main St., Loa, UT 84747, (435) 836-2811.
• *Fishlake National Forest Backcountry Guide for Hiking and Horseback Riding*, by M. Biddle, Wasatch, 1993.

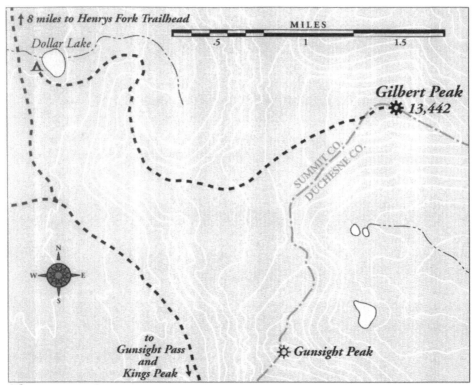

↑ 8 miles to Henrys Fork Trailhead

Dollar Lake

MILES

.5   1   1.5

Gilbert Peak
☼ 13,442

SUMMIT CO.
DUCHESNE CO.

N W E S

to
Gunsight Pass
and
Kings Peak

☼ *Gunsight Peak*

* Contours are approximate

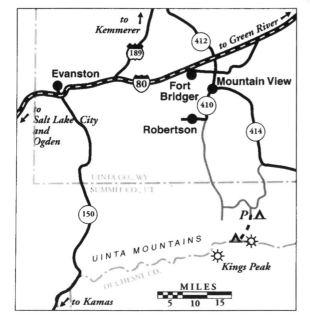

to
Kemmerer

(412)   to Green River →

(189)

Evanston

(80)

**Fort
Bridger**

Mountain View

to
Salt Lake City
and
Ogden

(410)

Robertson

(414)

UINTA CO., WY
SUMMIT CO., UT

(150)

P ▲

UINTA MOUNTAINS

▲ ☼

DUCHESNE CO.

☼

Kings Peak

MILES

5   10   15

↙ to Kamas

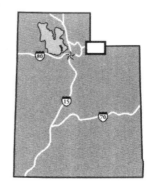

▬ ▬ ▬ ▬	Route
▬(235)▬	Secondary Road
▬▬▬	Dirt Road
··············	4WD Road
▬(89)▬	US Highway
▬(15)▬	Interstate
–·–·–	Stream
▲	Campground
☼	Summit
P	Parking

50

Gilbert Peak*

13,442 feet
Summit County

Time: 4.5–5.5 hours ~~~~ 2.25–2.75 hours

Distance: 5.75 miles

Difficulty: Difficult

Starting Elevation: 10,785 feet

Elevation Gain: 2,657 feet

USGS Maps: Mount Powell and Kings Peak

➤ Trailhead and Camping

Use the Henrys Fork trailhead as described for Kings Peak. Hike to Dollar Lake using the same trail description.

➤ Tips and Precautions

Because there is no trail from Dollar Lake to the summit, we highly recommend a map and compass. Because of the proximity of Gilbert Peak to Kings Peak, hikers might want to combine Gilbert and Kings into one long weekend trip, using Dollar Lake as a base camp.

THE WEST FLANK OF GILBERT PEAK

*The distance, times, difficulty, and other information pertaining to Gilbert Peak were based on the hike from Dollar Lake. See Kings Peak (page 59) for trail information from Henrys Fork trailhead to Dollar Lake.

MIKE MAKES HIS WAY UP THE FIRST PART OF THE RIDGE

➤ The Hike

Circle around the south side of Dollar Lake and traverse northeast around the hillside east of the lake. This is a very steep hillside, which is the western shoulder of a ridge that forms a cirque in the cliffs. Shortly after rounding that shoulder, start climbing right/south

THE VIEW LOOKING NORTH INTO WYOMING

up its northeast flank to the ridge. This is the steepest part of the hike.

Once on top of the ridge, follow it south and then east around the top of the cirque. This ridge offers spectacular views of the Henrys Fork basin as well as looking down into the amphitheater. One also has a commanding view of Kings Peak from this ridge.

Leave the ridge that forms the cirque as it starts to wind back to the north. Gilbert Peak is to the east, across meadows and boulder fields. After several false summits, the peak is marked by a small rock shelter.

➤ Background

Gilbert is the highest peak in Summit County and the second highest peak in the state, but there's no trail to its summit and it is seldom climbed. Its neighbor, Kings Peak, gets all of the attention. Kings Peak, the tallest mountain in the state, is 3.5 miles away.

The mountain was named after Grove Karl Gilbert, a geologist of the 1871–75 George Montague Wheeler survey and 1875–79 John Wesley Powell survey.

➤ For More Information

• Wasatch-Cache National Forest, Mountain View Ranger District, Lone Tree Road/Highway 44, Mountain View, WY 82939, (307) 782-6555.

• *High Uinta Trails*, by Mel Davis and John Veranth, Wasatch, 1993.

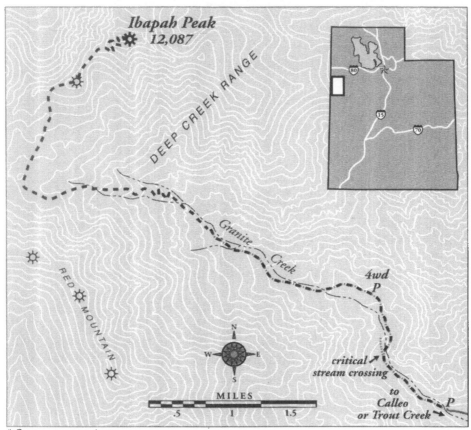

* Contours are approximate

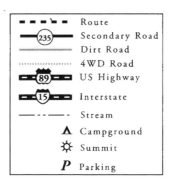

* No services available

Ibapah Peak
12,087 feet
Juab County

Time: 🐢 11–12.5 hours 🐇 6–7.5 hours

Distance: 14 miles

Difficulty: Extreme

Starting Elevation: 6,160 feet

Elevation Gain: 5,927 feet

USGS Maps: Ibapah Creek and Indian Farm Creek

➤ Trailhead
• From Callao, drive south 10.2 miles to a road on the right/west leading to Granite Creek Canyon. In 1997, there was a broken sign here that could be read only on the north-facing side.
• Drive 1 mile west, toward the canyon, until you reach a fork in the road. Take the left fork.
• Continue for another 2.8 miles, until a stream crosses the road. Most 2-wheel-drive vehicles should stop here.
• If you have a 4-wheel-drive vehicle and the crossing doesn't look too bad, continue up the road for another 0.8 mile. A road drops immediately off to the right and crosses the stream again. This is an easy junction to miss, so keep your eyes open for it.
• If you make it across the second stream crossing, continue up the road looking for a good place to camp. (We recommend stopping about 0.7 mile beyond the second stream crossing. This area provides some good camping spots and is possibly where motor vehicles are supposed to stop, but the sign was removed before 1997.) If you hike from here, you save 3 miles and 720 feet of climbing.

➤ Camping
There are several good car camping spots along the road leading into Granite Creek Canyon. There are no drinking water or restroom facilities.

➤ Tips and Precautions
Don't miss the right turn on the road at the second stream crossing! This is a very long and difficult hike—even more difficult if you start in the wrong place.There are no gas stations near the trailhead. Be sure to get gas before you leave the freeway.

RED MOUNTAIN

➤ The Hike

From wherever you decide to park, follow the road for a few miles as it winds up into the canyon. (If you hike from the first stream crossing, do not miss the right turn at the second stream crossing.) This road ends in a clearing where the trail climbs up to the left/west.

The steep hike climbs westward, with few switchbacks. Occasionally, the trail disappears in clearings that have been used as campsites. Keep an eye open for any small cairns that may have been placed along the route. Eventually, the trail ends in a large open Alpine meadow in the saddle below the granite-white Ibapah, the highest point visible on the right/north and the aptly named Red Mountain on the left/south. Turn right and cross the lower portion of this meadow. There is no trail.

Aim for the saddle on the ridge to the left of the foreground peak, which is on the left side of Ibapah. This portion of the route brings hikers above timberline. From the ridge, climb up the foreground peak and over to the back side. The route from here to Ibapah Peak looks ominous, but there's a trail that leads to the summit. The summit is marked by the remains of several rock shelters that were used by surveying crews.

When descending, you can catch a hardly discernible trail that skirts around to the south flank of the foreground peak—saving you the trouble of climbing back up it. But be careful. If you miss the route, possibly because of snow covering the trail, you could end up dropping down and climbing up a series of drainages on the peak's southeast flank.

➤ Background

Ibapah Peak is perhaps the most remote of all Utah's county high peaks. It is located at the far western edge of the state in the Deep Creek Mountains, south of Wendover and north of nowhere.

GRANITE BOULDERS ALONG THE ROUTE TO THE SUMMIT

The Utah Wilderness Coalition in *Wilderness at the Edge* described the Deep Creek Mountains this way: "The enormous vertical relief—greater than that of the Teton Range from Jackson Hole—creates a variety of ecological conditions that foster biological diversity unmatched in Utah's desert mountains."

Ibapah was named after the town of Ibapah, on the northwest side of the mountain range. According to John Van Cott's *Utah Place Names*, it was originally called Deep Creek after the nearby river—hence, the name of the range. The town name was changed to Ibapah after the Goshute Indian word meaning "white clay water." Goshutes still live in the shadow of Ibapah Peak, with their reservation on the western flank of the Deep Creek range.

➤ For More Information
  • *Wilderness at the Edge*, by the Utah Wilderness Coalition, 1992.

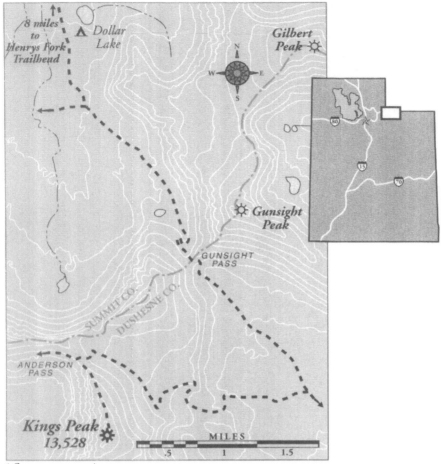

8 miles to Henrys Fork Trailhead

△ *Dollar Lake*

Gilbert Peak ☼

N
W · E
S

☼ *Gunsight Peak*

GUNSIGHT PASS

SUMMIT CO.
DUCHESNE CO.

ANDERSON PASS

Kings Peak 13,528 ✶

MILES
.5   1   1.5

* *Contours are approximate*

to Kemmerer

412

to Green River

189

Evanston

80

Fort Bridger

Mountain View

410

414

to Salt Lake City and Ogden

Robertson

UINTA CO., WY
SUMMIT CO., UT

150

P △

△ ☼ *Gilbert Peak*

☼

UINTA MOUNTAINS

to Kamas

DUCHESNE CO.

MILES
5   10   15

- - - -	Route
235	Secondary Road
	Dirt Road
··········	4WD Road
89	US Highway
15	Interstate
- · - · -	Stream
△	Campground
☼	Summit
P	Parking

58

Kings Peak
13,528 feet
Duchesne County

Time: 🐢 15–17 hours 🐰 9.5–10.5 hours

Distance: 30 miles

Difficulty: Extreme

Starting Elevation: 9,400 feet

Elevation Gain: 4,128 feet

USGS Maps: Kings Peak and Mount Powell

➤ Trailhead
• From Interstate 80 in Wyoming, 22 miles east of Evanston, turn south to Mountain View.
• In Mountain View turn right/west on Wyoming Highway 410, toward Robertson. This road soon bends left/south.
• After 7 miles, the paved road veers right/west toward Robertson. Continue straight/south onto a gravel road that leads to the Wasatch National Forest.
• Turn left after 12.3 miles, toward Henrys Fork.
• After 7 miles, turn right (which is actually straight, as the main road bends left) at the Henrys Fork sign.
• Continue another 3 miles to the campground. The trailhead is at the end of the farthest parking lot.

➤ Camping
Water and restroom facilities are available at Henrys Fork trailhead. There are several campsites, but they are often full because this is one of the busiest trailheads in the Uintas.

➤ Tips and Precautions
Kings Peak can be climbed from the Henrys Fork trailhead in one day, but that would be a very long, hard day. We recommend making the trek in a weekend, perhaps combining this hike with nearby Gilbert Peak. Camping near Dollar Lake makes a good starting point for both mountains.

Hikers have been known to cut across the meadow at the foot of the cliffs after crossing over Gunsight Pass on their way to Anderson Pass. This is unnecessary. We stuck to the trail and finished well ahead of others who took the so-called shortcut.

► The Hike

This well-established trail climbs gently, about 1,100 feet over 8 miles, along the Henrys Fork River to Dollar Lake. This is a good weekend backpacking trip for people who aren't necessarily interested in bagging a peak.

From the trailhead, the trail climbs along the edge of the river through the thick forest. Occasionally, the trail wanders through an Alpine meadow, lush with wildflowers and wildlife. Moose are a common sight along this drainage.

After about 5.5 miles, the trail reaches a junction at Elkhorn Crossing. You don't want to miss the junction. Cut back left down the stream bank and across a rickety log bridge that spans the creek. Once on the other side, continue hiking south along the creek. Eventually, the trail

CROSSING THE FOOT BRIDGE

climbs out of the forest and into an open basin. A small stream from Dollar Lake usually trickles across the trail just before it reaches the trees that surround the lake. This is a well-used camping area for hikers aiming to stand atop Utah's highest peak.

From Dollar Lake, the trail continues southeast and gently climbs above timberline. It reaches into a small canyon at the base of Gunsight Pass, 11,888 feet, before it starts switchbacking up the right side. After crossing the pass, the trail winds down into Painter Basin east of Kings Peak. It stretches far out into this flat meadow before it reaches a junction and cuts back to the right toward Anderson Pass, where it again starts to climb, winding its way north along Kings' eastern flank. From Anderson Pass, 12,680 feet, the trail becomes faint as it climbs into the large boulders that comprise the summit. Scramble south up the ridge to the peak, which is marked by a plaque.

A scree and talus chute near Anderson Pass offers a tempting, quick descent toward Dollar Lake after leaving the summit, but this chute has deteriorated over the years and has become quite dangerous. It should be used only if a hasty retreat is necessary to escape dangerous weather.

THE LAST SCRAMBLE TO THE TOP

MIKE DROPS FROM GUNSIGHT PASS INTO PAINTER BASIN

KINGS PEAK CAN BE SEEN IN THE DISTANCE FROM HENRYS FORK BASIN

➤ Background

Because Kings Peak is the highest in Utah, its summit is the goal of count-less Boy Scouts and other hikers—trained and untrained—from across Utah.

Kings Peak was named after Clarence King, a geologist and surveyor who explored the Uintas between 1868 and 1871 and later became director of the U.S. Geological Survey. In 1864, while working with a California Geological Survey party in the Sierras, King had named the highest peak in the contiguous 48 states after his boss, Josiah Whitney, but he failed to be the first person to climb the lofty peak after three attempts in which he climbed the wrong mountains.

➤ For More Information
   • Wasatch-Cache National Forest, Mountain View Ranger District, Lone Tree Road/Highway 44, Mountain View, WY 82939, (307) 782-6555.
   • *Hiking Utah*, by Dave Hall, Falcon, 1997.
   • *High Uinta Trails*, by Mel Davis and John Veranth, Wasatch, 1993.

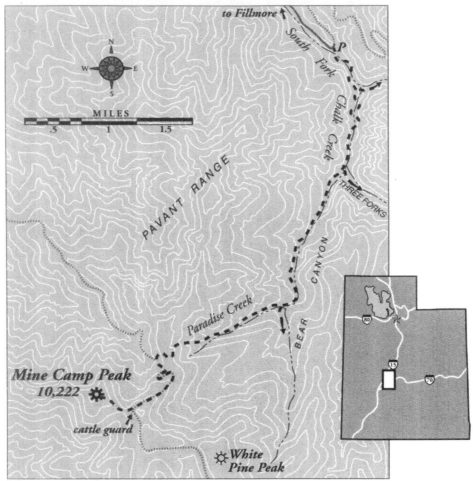

to Fillmore

South Fork

Chalk Creek

P

THREE FORKS

PAVANT RANGE

BEAR CANYON

Paradise Creek

Mine Camp Peak
10,222 ☼

cattle guard

☼ **White Pine Peak**

MILES

.5   1   1.5

N
W   E
S

* *Contours are approximate*

to Delta

to Nephi

50

28

50

89

MILES

5   10   15

Fillmore

P
☼

KANOSH NATION

15

PAVANT RANGE

Salina

89

to Green River

Richfield

70

24

MILLARD CO.

SANPETE CO.

SEVIER CO.

PIUTE CO.

to Beaver

to Loa

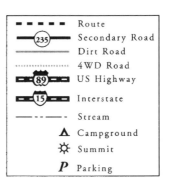

▬ ▬ ▬	Route
━235━	Secondary Road
─────	Dirt Road
··········	4WD Road
89	US Highway
15	Interstate
─·─·─	Stream
▲	Campground
☼	Summit
P	Parking

Mine Camp Peak
10,222 feet
Millard County

Time:  7.75–9 hours   4–5.75 hours

Distance: 12 miles

Difficulty: Difficult

Starting Elevation: 6,440 feet

Elevation Gain: 3,782 feet

USGS Maps: Sunset Peak, Mt. Catherine, White Pine Peak, and Fillmore

➤ Trailhead

• From Main Street in Fillmore, head east on 200 South, which becomes Chalk Creek Road.

• After 9.5 miles, the road turns switchbacks to the left while a spur continues up the canyon just beyond a picnic site. The Bear Canyon/Pine Creek Trail trailhead is just a few hundred feet up the canyon where the road ends along the river.

➤ Camping

Camping is not allowed at the picnic areas along the creek. However, you can find a suitable place to car camp along the creek near the trailhead.

➤ Tips and precautions

Be prepared for several stream crossings during the first couple of miles along the trail. We recommend wearing sandals until reaching a point about a mile up Bear Canyon, then changing into boots. Also, be ready for a difficult off-trail climb up Paradise Canyon and a haul up the steep headwall above the canyon.

THE LAST STRETCH OF ROAD

65

MIKE LEAPS OVER A STREAM   AND ANOTHER STREAM CROSSING

➤ The Hike

Hikers will get up close and personal with the river as they cross it numerous times where the trail, which was once an old mining road, meanders up the first canyon. The trail reaches a junction with the Bear Canyon Trail 1 mile beyond the trailhead. Take a right and hike south along the Bear Canyon Trail. The trail is steep in a few places as it occasionally climbs above the river into the maples, oaks, and mountain mahogany. A few waterfalls cascade into this canyon, providing breathtaking sights under the forest canopy. Keep your eyes open for remnants of the mining activity that once flourished here.

Most of this section of the hike is along Chalk Creek, which you will follow until it eventually veers left where it flows down from the top of Bear Canyon. Continue right and up the drainage beyond Bear Canyon, which is Paradise Canyon. This is where the route gets a bit tricky and a topographic map is essential. The trail becomes faint and mostly nonexistent after it climbs up away from the river and crosses a meadow. Find a route up this gully. It might be easier to walk in the streambed if there is little or no water in it.

Evan Hanson, who climbed Utah's county high peaks in 1997 with his son Ty, said a trail may be found on the southeast ridge, or left side, above this gully. It starts where Paradise and Bear canyons intersect.

Eventually, if you stay down in the Paradise Canyon gully, the route reaches a steep headwall. Aim for a notch in the saddle as you climb this steep slope. Lucky hikers may get a chance to "talk" to a golden eagle in the patches of trees along this hillside. Once on top, walk left/south-southeast until you catch a

AND ANOTHER

AND ANOTHER

dirt road. This road will wind around to a ridgeline that drops off to the right and leads up to Mine Camp Peak. The jumping-off point from the road is just before reaching a cattle guard.

There is no distinct trail down the saddle and up to the peak. But the route-finding is fairly easy. A large cairn marks the summit.

➤ Background

Mine Camp Peak is in the Fishlake National Forest and, more specifically, the Pavant Mountains, which were named by Native Americans for the water flowing from them. But the upper reaches of the range are arid compared to the lower reaches, which are filled with creeks and rivers.

If you're lucky, you might catch a glimpse of the mountain lions that are reportedly abundant in the Pavants.

➤ For More Information
  • Fishlake National Forest, Fillmore Ranger District, 390 S. Main St., Fillmore, UT 84631, (435) 743-5721.
  • *Fishlake National Forest Backcountry Guide for Hiking and Horseback Riding*, by M. Biddle, Wasatch, 1993.

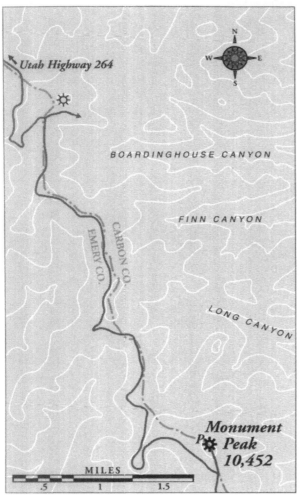

Utah Highway 264

BOARDINGHOUSE CANYON

FINN CANYON

EMERY CO.

CARBON CO.

LONG CANYON

Monument
P Peak
10,452

MILES
.5   1   1.5

* Contours are approximate

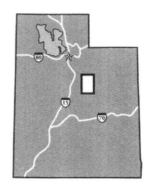

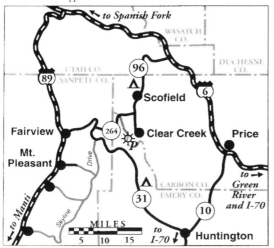

to Spanish Fork

WASATCH
CO.

UTAH CO.
SANPETE CO.

DUCHESNE
CO.

89

96

Scofield

6

Fairview

264

Clear Creek

Price

Mt.
Pleasant

Drive

to Manti

Skyline

CARBON CO.
EMERY CO.

to
Green
River
and I-70

31

10

MILES
5   10   15

to
I-70

Huntington

Monument Peak
10,452 feet
Carbon County

Time: —

Distance: —

Difficulty: Too Easy

Starting Elevation: 10,452 feet

Elevation Gain: —

USGS Maps: Scofield and Candland Mountain

➤ Trailhead
• Just southeast of Soldier Summit on U.S. Highway 6 between Spanish Fork and Price, turn west onto Utah Highway 96.
• Drive to Scofield and continue past the town.
• About 4 miles before reaching Clear Creek, take a right on Utah Highway 31/264.
• Drive to the county line and take a left, heading south.
• Drive 5.2 miles and take a left at a junction in the road marked by a sign describing a gate in 300 feet.
• Continue for 2.7 miles and take another left, which is a hairpin turn of sorts, cutting back north to the summit.

➤ Camping
   Camping may be available at the nearby lakes and reservoirs. Flat Canyon Campground is located near Utah Highway 31/264, west of Electric Lake. The campground has drinking water and restroom facilities, and it charges a fee.

➤ Tips and Precautions
   Bring a mountain bike or plan to do something besides hiking. Roads leading to Carbon County's highest peak can get slick and treacherous with just a little bit of rainfall, so check weather forecasts before driving to this summit.

ATOP THE SUMMIT

THE ROAD LEADING TO THE RADIO TOWER ON THE SUMMIT

DAN TRIES TO GAIN MORE ELEVATION

PHOTO BY MICHAEL R. WEIBEL

> ## The Hike

This isn't a hike. It's a drive. The summit is marked by a large cairn near a hut and radio tower.

> ## Background

Monument Peak, East Mountain, and South Tent Mountain are all on top of the Wasatch Plateau, which forms the western edge of the San Rafael Swell. In the 1930s, crews from the Civilian Conservation Corps and Work Projects Administration completed the 100-mile-long Skyline Drive that crosses the plateau. The road can be used to combine hikes to all three peaks.

For its length, Skyline Drive is one of the highest roads in the United States. The road provides magnificent views of Sanpete Valley, mile-deep canyons, lake-filled basins, and sub-Alpine meadow and forests. It is a dirt road and rough in places. People who travel it should do so in good weather. Some sections are best driven only by high-clearance 4-wheel-drive vehicles.

> ## For More Information

• Manti-La Sal National Forest, Price Ranger District, 599 W. Price River Drive, Price, UT 84501, (435) 637-2817.

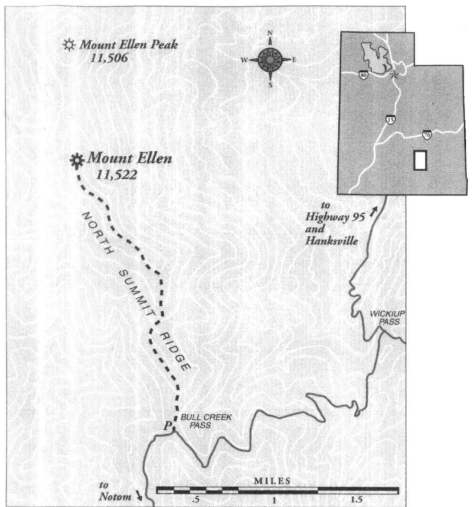

☼ *Mount Ellen Peak*
11,506

N
W — E
S

to
Highway 95
and
Hanksville ↑

☼ *Mount Ellen*
11,522

NORTH SUMMIT RIDGE

WICKIUP
PASS

BULL CREEK
PASS

P

to
Notom ↓

MILES
.5   1   1.5

* Contours are approximate

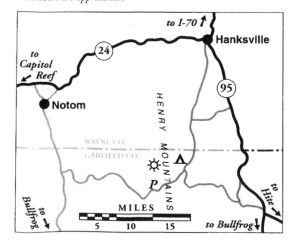

to I-70 ↑

24   Hanksville

to
Capitol
Reef ↙

95

● Notom

HENRY MOUNTAINS

WAYNE CO.
GARFIELD CO.

☼
△

P

to
Hite ↘

to
Bullfrog ↓

MILES
5   10   15

to Bullfrog ↓

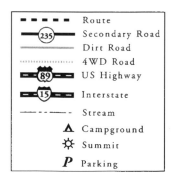

▬ ▬ ▬ ▬   Route
━235━   Secondary Road
━━━━   Dirt Road
·········   4WD Road
━89━   US Highway
━15━   Interstate
— · —   Stream
△   Campground
☼   Summit
P   Parking

Mount Ellen

11,522 feet
Garfield County

Time: 🐢 2–3 hours   🐇 1–1.75 hours

Distance: 4 miles

Difficulty: Easy

Starting Elevation: 10,485 feet

Elevation Gain: 1,037 feet

USGS Map: Mount Ellen

➤ Trailhead
• Drive south from Hanksville on Utah Highway 95 for 10 miles.
• Turn right/west onto Sawmill Basin Road.
• Drive 6 miles to an intersection. Take a left/south.
• Drive 9.5 miles to Lonesome Beaver Campground.
• From the campground, continue up the hill another 1.7 miles to a junction. Take a right/west to Bullcreek Pass.
• Drive 2.8 miles to the pass. An obvious trail starts on the right and follows the ridge to the summit.

➤ Camping
Lonesome Beaver Campground is a great place to stay before or after the hike. It's close to the trailhead and, because of its remote location, likely to have a vacant spot. McMillan Springs Campground is on the other side of the pass. Both have restrooms, and Lonesome Beaver has drinking water.

➤ Tips and Precautions
The drive probably takes more out of a person than the hike. It's a long, dirt road. We recommend a 4-wheel-drive vehicle, but a 2-wheel-drive vehicle with high clearance can make the trip if the driver is patient.

The Henry Mountains are very remote and BLM personnel do not make regular patrols of the area. You may not meet anyone else on the road if you run into trouble, so be prepared for any contingency.

THE HIGHEST PEAK ON THE MOUNT ELLEN RIDGE IS THE MIDDLE BUMP

➤ The Hike

The trailhead at Bull Creek Pass is often blocked by snowdrifts until late July. From the pass, a well-defined trail leads north along the ridge across three minor peaks before reaching the summit of Ellen.

The summit is the highest point on the volcanic dome that forms Mount Ellen. Mount Ellen Peak, on the other hand, is a pyramid-shaped peak farther north of the summit, and it is lower than its neighbor with a similar name.

Most of the hike is above timberline and can be surprisingly hot and dry.

Several rock shelters comprise the boulder-strewn summit, which provides a commanding view of southern Utah including the Aquarius Plateau, the Abajo and La Sal mountains, and the colorful Capital Reef National Park.

➤ Background

The Henry Mountains, which rise high above the surrounding desert, were the last mountains in the contiguous 48 states to be mapped. During John Wesley Powell's first expedition down the Colorado River, they were noted on maps as the Unknown Mountains. In 1869, during Powell's second expedition on the river, the mountains were named after noted physicist Joseph Henry of the Smithsonian Institution, an active supporter of Powell's expeditions. At the same time, Powell named one of the peaks in the range after his sister Ellen— who was also the wife of Powell's field director, Almon Thompson.

Gold was discovered in the 1890s on the high eastern slope of Ellen. One small building in Eagle City, southeast of Bull Creek Pass, stands as a reminder of the small amount of prospecting that took place in the Henry Mountains.

Outlaws like Butch Cassidy and the Sundance Kid spent a lot of time around the Henry Mountains, hiding in nearby Robber's Roost along the Dirty Devil River. Their prey, cattle, still graze around the mountain.

Keep an eye out for bison. In 1941, 18 head of bison were transplanted here from Yellowstone National Park. The herd, according to BLM publications, is one of the few free-roaming and huntable herds of American bison in the contiguous 48 states. Today, the herd includes more than 200 animals. Approximately 44 permits are issued each year to hunt the bison.

➤ For More Information
• BLM/Henry Mountain Resource Area, 406 S.

ABOVE BULL CREEK PASS

100 West, Hanksville, UT 84734, (435) 542-3461. (They have a couple of publications available, including a general recreation map of the Henry Mountains and a brochure detailing the 56-mile Bull Creek Pass National Back Country Byway.)
• *Hiking and Exploring Utah's Henry Mountains and Robber's Roost*, by Michael Kelsey, Kelsey Publishing Co., 1987.

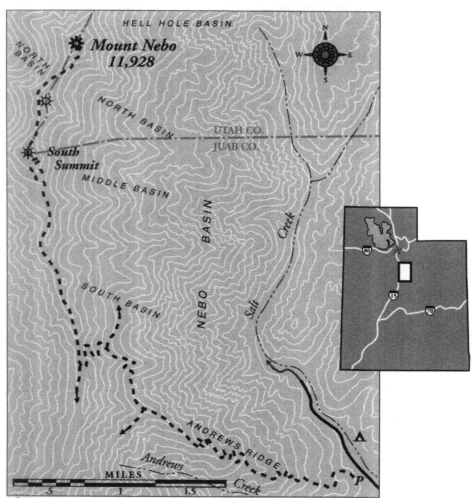

HELL HOLE BASIN

NORTH BASIN

Mount Nebo
11,928

NORTH BASIN

UTAH CO.
JUAB CO.

South Summit

MIDDLE BASIN

NEBO BASIN

Salt Creek

SOUTH BASIN

ANDREWS RIDGE

Andrews Creek

P

MILES

.5   1   1.5

* *Contours are approximate*

Utah Lake

to Provo

Spanish Fork

Santaquin

Payson

Nebo Loop Road

6

to Delta

6

to Price

15

89

to Price

UTAH CO.
SANPETE CO.

P

Nephi

#225 Exit

JUAB CO.

132

to Fillmore

to Highway 89

Fairview

to Ephraim

31

MILES

5

10

15

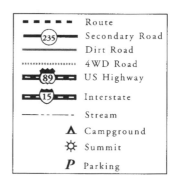

- - - - - Route
━235━ Secondary Road
───── Dirt Road
·······89······· 4WD Road
▭89▭ US Highway
▭15▭ Interstate
─·─·─ Stream
▲ Campground
☼ Summit
P Parking

Mount Nebo

11,928 feet
Utah County

Time:  12–14 hours 7–8.5 hours

Distance: 11 miles

Difficulty: Extreme

Starting Elevation: 6,520 feet

Elevation Gain: 5,408 feet

USGS Maps: Nebo Basin and Mona

➤ Trailhead
• From Interstate 15, take Nephi exit 225 and drive east on Utah Highway 132 for approximately 4.5 miles.
• Take a left/north on the Nebo Loop Road.
• Drive 3.3 miles and take another left.
• Drive 1.3 miles to the trailhead, which is in a parking area on the left.

➤ Camping
 Bear Canyon and Ponderosa campgrounds have drinking water and restroom facilities. Both charge fees.

➤ Tips and Precautions
 This is probably the most difficult hike of Utah's county high points. The hike averages nearly 1,000 feet of elevation gained per mile for more than 5 miles, and there's some nasty scrambling across the knife-edge ridge to the north peak. If you're uncomfortable with this precarious scramble, you might want to turn around after reaching the south summit.

MOUNT NEBO SKYLINE FROM I-15

► The Hike

From the trailhead, the route climbs through maple and oak thickets to a ridge above Andrews Canyon on the left/south. Ascend this ridge, hiking into the aspens and conifers. Eventually, the trail wanders right/north away from Andrews Canyon. Along this section of the trail, you can see the three Nebo summits towering above you to the north. Continue along the trail to a point just below the south ridge, where a series of long switchbacks heads up to the ridge. Here, the trail climbs about 600 feet in 0.5 mile to a saddle.

Turn right/north and follow the ridge through limber pines to the 11,877-foot south summit. A sign placed by the Wasatch Mountain Club marks this peak, but it's not the highest one.

UNDER THE MIDDLE SUMMIT

There are three options at this point. First, you can call it quits here and return to the trailhead. Second, you can follow the knife-edge ridge for 1 mile over the middle peak to the north summit. Third, you can drop down to the west just a bit and traverse along the ridge on some very loose scree to the north summit.

A faint trail can be seen at times along both the ridge and the traverse. The traverse is exposed in a few places, and it occasionally climbs back up to the ridge. If you choose the lower route along the top of the scree, you might want to climb back to a saddle along the ridge after traversing past the middle summit. A good, but not obvious, trail runs along the east side of the ridge from here to the north summit.

Once you reach the north peak, you will have spectacular views to both sides of the range, as well as to the north where you can see much of the Wasatch Mountains towering over the Salt Lake Valley.

► Background

Contrary to what many people believe, Mount Timpanogos, our Utah Classic overlooking Provo, is not the highest peak in Utah County. Mount Nebo, east of Nephi, is the highest peak in both Utah County and all of the Wasatch Mountains. It was likely named by Mormon pioneers after the biblical Mount Nebo in the Old Testament. That mountain was the highest peak above the Jordan River in Moab, where Moses died.

Three major peaks comprise the summit of Nebo, the highest of which is the north summit. A long, steep, well-established trail leads to the south sum-

MIKE CLIMBS UP THE MIDDLE SUMMIT

mit. From there, hikers must either negotiate a knife-edge ridge or try their luck at scrambling over very loose scree on the traverse to the north summit.

➤ For More Information
• Uinta National Forest, Spanish Fork Ranger District, 44 W. 400 North, Spanish Fork, UT 84660, (801) 798-3571.
• *Hiking Utah*, by Dave Hall, Falcon, 1997.

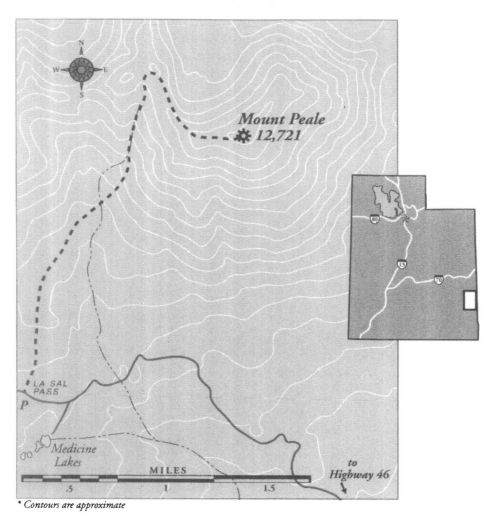

Mount Peale
☀ 12,721

LA SAL
PASS

P

Medicine
Lakes

MILES

.5 1 1.5

to
Highway 46

* Contours are approximate

Mount ☀
Tukuhnikivatz ☀

La Sal
Pass
P

MILES
1 2 3

☀ South
Mountain

to Moab

La Sal
Junction

46

La Sal

to
Colorado
and
Highway 90

191

to Monticello

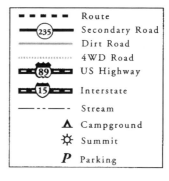

▬ ▬ ▬ ▬	Route
▬235▬	Secondary Road
▬▬▬	Dirt Road
··········	4WD Road
▬89▬	US Highway
▬15▬	Interstate
—·—·—	Stream
▲	Campground
☀	Summit
P	Parking

Mount Peale

12,721 feet
San Juan County

Time: 5–6 hours  2–2.5 hours

Distance: 5 miles

Difficulty: Difficult

Starting Elevation: 10,125 feet

Elevation Gain: 2,596 feet

USGS Map: Mount Peale

➤ Trailhead

• From the McDonald's restaurant in Moab, drive south on U.S. Highway 191 for 21.8 miles to La Sal Junction. Turn left/east on Utah Highway 46.

• Drive 12.8 miles and turn left/north off the paved road. Follow the signs to La Sal Pass.

• Drive 2 miles and take another left.

• Continue for 7.4 miles to the pass.

➤ Camping

There are no improved camp-grounds near the trailhead. However, there are several good spots for car camping near the pass.

➤ Tips and Precautions

This is a very steep hike, averaging 1,038 feet of elevation per mile. It can be quite dangerous in the chute if it is still filled with snow and ice. You might carry an ice ax and crampons on this hike to use if the chute is particularly nasty.

JOSÉ KNIGHTON DESCENDS THE RIDGE

► The Hike

There is no trail to the top of Mount Peale, but most of the route can be seen from the pass.

Hike north across the meadow, aiming for a steep couloir on the west flank of the mountain that heads up to a saddle along the ridge. To get to this drainage, you must hike through a fairly dense forest of aspens and evergreens. Maintain the same bearing through the trees so you'll emerge at the base of the couloir.

The talus gully is narrow and steep. It can be hazardous with or without snow.

Once on top of the saddle, turn right/southeast and follow the ridgecrest as it wraps around to the rocky summit.

► Background

HALFWAY UP THE GULLY

"The imposing presence of the La Sals, towering above canyon country, conveys an initial impression of dominance. The Olympian summits of Utah's second highest range reign over their surrounding canyons," according to José Knighton, in his book *Canyon Country's La Sal Mountains Hiking and Nature Handbook*.

Their name, meaning the salt mountains, was given to the La Sals in 1776 by Spanish explorers who may not have believed the white caps were snow in the middle of summer atop this desert range. They knew salt deposits were numerous in this area, but it was indeed snow that covered the mountains.

Mount Peale was named for Albert Peale, a mineralogist on Ferdinand Hayden's 1875 survey team.

A yellow rayless daisy is quite abundant on top of Peale and its neighboring La Sal peaks. Knighton explained that the La Sal daisy, *Erigeron mancus*, is found nowhere else in the world. "If this rather innocuous flower were not so common across the range's summits, ridges and high slopes, it would certainly qualify for threatened or endangered status," he said.

MIKE CAREFULLY GLISSADES DOWN THE GULLY

➤ For More Information
• Manti-La Sal National Forest, Moab Ranger District, 2290 S. West
Resource Blvd., Moab, UT 84532, (435) 259-7155.
• *Canyon Country's La Sal Mountains Hiking and Nature Handbook*, by José
Knighton, Canyon Country Publications, 1995.

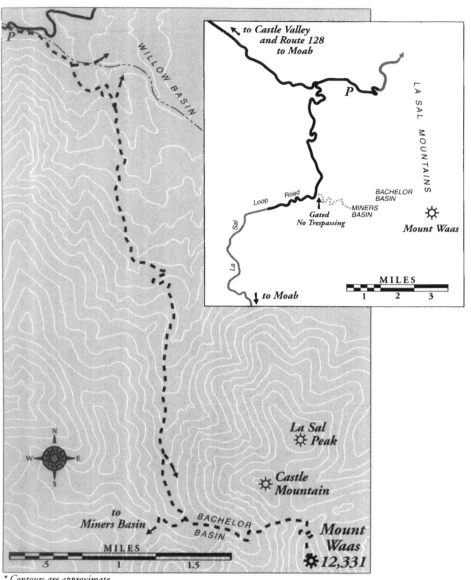

* Contours are approximate

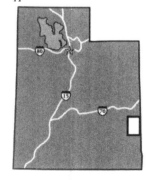

Legend

▪ ▪ ▪ ▪	Route
━(235)━	Secondary Road
────	Dirt Road
·········	4WD Road
━(89)━	US Highway
━(15)━	Interstate
─ · ─ · ─	Stream
▲	Campground
☼	Summit
P	Parking

Map labels: WILLOW BASIN, LA SAL MOUNTAINS, to Castle Valley and Route 128 to Moab, P, BACHELOR BASIN, MINERS BASIN, Gated No Trespassing, Loop Road, La Sal, Mount Waas, to Moab, MILES 1 2 3, La Sal Peak, Castle Mountain, to Miners Basin, BACHELOR BASIN, Mount Waas 12,331, MILES .5 1 1.5, N E S W

Mount Waas

12,331 feet
Grand County

Time:  10–12 hours 5–6.5 hours
Distance: 10.75 miles
Difficulty: Extreme
Starting Elevation: 7,090 feet
Elevation Gain: 5,241 feet
USGS Maps: Mount Waas and Warner Lake

➤ Trailhead
• From 100 North in Moab, drive north on U.S. Highway 191 for 2.3 miles. Turn right/northeast on Utah Highway 128.
• Drive 15.7 miles and turn right, following signs to Castle Valley and the La Sal Loop Road.
• There's a junction in 10.7 miles. Continue driving straight/east for another 1.6 miles. Park near the cattle guard and corral.

➤ Camping
   There are no improved campgrounds near the trailhead. Oakgrove and Big Bend campgrounds are on Utah Highway 128, along the Colorado River, between Moab and the Castle Valley turnoff.

➤ Tips and Precautions
   Before 1997, the standard route for climbing Mount Waas was in Miner's Basin, but a gate has since been built on the road leading to that trailhead, which crosses through private property. A trail in Bachelor Basin approaches the mountain from the north. It is a longer route, but its access doesn't cut across private property.
   There are several junctions along this trail. We highly recommend a map and compass.

AN EXTRAORDINARY VIEW TO THE SOUTH

RORY TYLER STANDS ON THE SADDLE NORTH OF THE SUMMIT

➤ The Hike

From the trailhead, the trail leads southeast along Castle Creek. After about 0.75 mile, mostly on a 2-track trail, a single-track trail branches off to the right and starts climbing south, away from the creek and into the forest.

The single-track trail eventually reaches another junction with a 2-track trail in the dense forest. Turn right at this junction and start climbing this wide trail.

As this trail approaches the base of Castle Mountain, a narrow trail forks off to the right side of the wider trail. If you miss this fork, you can catch the new route farther down the trail at a morainelike rock glacier. Simply move right into the trees at this point and catch the single-track trail that works its way around the rock pile. Farther up the canyon, the trail may become difficult to read and several animal trails crisscross the main route. Look for cairns and tree blazes, and stay near the central portion of the drainage.

The trail bends hard to the right/west after the junction of trails between Miner's Basin and Bachelor's Basin. The old road leading into Bachelor Basin was obscured in 1997 by deadfall and avalanche debris. Find the route as it runs left/east up the basin.

The remnants of several old miners' cabins are scattered along the trail.

The trail emerges from the forest at the foot of Mount Waas. Find a route that climbs steeply along the left/north side of a narrow talus gully. There may be a number of animal trails here to help hikers make a series of switchbacks to

THE FINAL STEEP TALUS SLOPE

AN OLD CABIN IN BACHELOR BASIN

DIANE BUSH ASCENDS THE NORTH SHOULDER

the saddle between Mount Waas and Castle Mountain. From this large saddle, a well-established trail climbs through the talus to the top of Mount Waas.

➤ Background

Mount Waas was named by men on Ferdinand Hayden's 1875 survey team, but there are conflicting reports about the name's origin. One story attributes it to a Ute chief. Another story attributes the name to one of Hayden's native guides.

José Knighton, in his book *Canyon Country's La Sal Mountains Hiking and Nature Handbook*, said this trail is one of the few in the La Sals that passes through the full spectrum of the range's habitats. It starts in oak and ponderosa pine. After a lengthy climb, it arrives in a glacial basin at a relic mine camp below Mount Waas.

➤ For More Information
• Manti-La Sal National Forest, Moab Ranger District, 2290 S. West Resource Blvd., Moab, UT 84532, (435) 259-7155.
• *Canyon Country's La Sal Mountains Hiking and Nature Handbook*, by José Knighton, Canyon Country Publications, 1995.

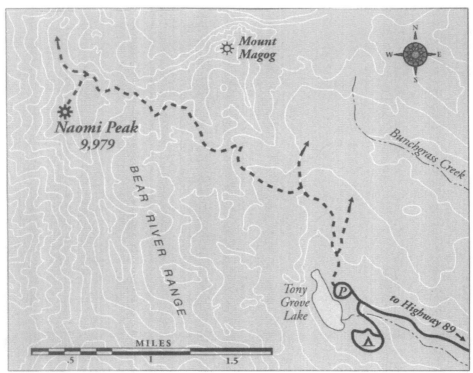

Mount Magog

Naomi Peak
9,979

BEAR RIVER RANGE

Bunchgrass Creek

Tony Grove Lake

to Highway 89

P

MILES

.5   1   1.5

* Contours are approximate

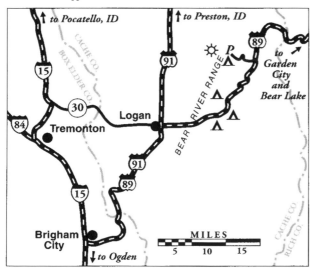

to Pocatello, ID

to Preston, ID

89

91

CACHE CO.
BOX ELDER CO.

15

to Garden City and Bear Lake

BEAR RIVER RANGE

30

Logan

84

Tremonton

91

89

15

89

Brigham City

to Ogden

CACHE CO.
RICH CO.

MILES

5   10   15

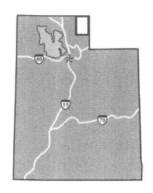

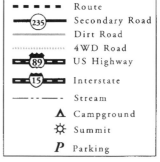

	Route
235	Secondary Road
	Dirt Road
	4WD Road
89	US Highway
15	Interstate
	Stream
▲	Campground
☼	Summit
P	Parking

Naomi Peak

9,979 feet
Cache County

Time:  3–4 hours   1.5–2 hours
Distance: 8 miles
Difficulty: Moderate
Starting Elevation: 8,029 feet
Elevation Gain: 1,950 feet
USGS Map: Naomi Peak

➤ Trailhead
• From Logan, drive east on 400 North (U.S. Highway 89). Logan Canyon starts where the highway crosses Logan River, just past Utah State University.
• Drive 19.5 miles into the canyon. Turn left, following signs to Tony Grove Lake. A paved road winds 7 miles from the highway to the lake.
• Beyond the backcountry parking lot and the campground, the road ends in a loop-shaped parking lot on the east side of the lake. The trail starts on the right side, at the end of the loop, and climbs the small hillside overlooking the parking lot.

➤ Camping
Tony Grove Lake Campground is located just before the parking lot loop. Another campground, Lewis M. Turner Campground, is located at the highway turnoff. Both have drinking water and restroom facilities. A fee is charged at Tony Grove campground.

➤ Tips and Precautions
Naomi is reached by a generally moderate hike climbing through several open meadows. There are less than a handful of steep sections in the hike, and each takes only a few minutes to climb. And, at the top of each steep section, there's a stand of trees—usually Engelmann spruce or Alpine fir—under which you can relax and take a break in the shade.

CHERRY PEAK AND CACHE VALLEY

➤ The Hike

Shortly after you start up the trail, in a matter of minutes, the trail splits at a large billboard. The sign includes a trail register and a map showing the Mount Naomi Wilderness Area, which lies just beyond the mountain's north-south ridgeline. Follow the trail on the left. In fact, always veer left whenever the trail forks beyond this point.

DIANE BUSH RETURNING TO THE SADDLE

The trail starts on a gentle slope, through various meadows and boulder fields. On the left, layers of quartzite form a set of steps, called the Giant's Stairway or Devil's Staircase, leading up the hillside. The unique outcropping is a result of glacial "plucking" as ice moved across the slope many years ago.

Past the staircase, the trail starts its first steep section as it climbs above the lighter colored quartzite and into the darker dolostone formations that are common throughout Logan Canyon. The trail winds through some small cliffs and up a gully before reaching the first small valley.

As the trail climbs into a second valley, hikers get their first glimpse of Naomi: the left of two adjacent rock outcroppings high atop the ridge.

At the ridge, the trail splits again. Following the contours on the left/south, hikers will get to use their hands as they maneuver over a few small boulders on their way to the summit. The rock outcropping that marks the peak offers a tremendous view of northern Utah. To the southeast, the Uintas stretch across the horizon. To the west, you can peer down into Smithfield Canyon and see the flat Cache Valley floor.

➤ Background

At 9,979 feet, Naomi is the highest peak in the Bear River Range, one of Utah's northernmost mountain ranges. The 70-mile-long range was named after the Bear River, which winds its way around the northern end of the mountains. The range separates Logan from the popular Bear Lake in neighboring Rich County.

Naomi was named in the 1870s by a government surveyor who was homesick for his wife. Tony Grove Lake got its name from the social elite who frequented the area in the 1880s. Today, it's a favorite recreation destination for many locals, serving as a trailhead for several hikes as well as a popular camping and fishing spot during the summer and a snowmobile and cross-country skiing haven during the winter.

Jack Greene, a seasonal forest ranger, said he's seen people in their 70s and

LOOKING OVER CACHE VALLEY FROM THE SUMMIT

80s reach the summit as well as very young children. It's a great hike for beginning and experienced hikers alike.

➤ For More Information
  • Wasatch-Cache National Forest, Logan Ranger District, 1500 E. Highway 89, Logan, UT 84321, (435) 755-3620.
  • *Cache Trails*, by John Wood, Bridgerland Audubon Society, 1994.

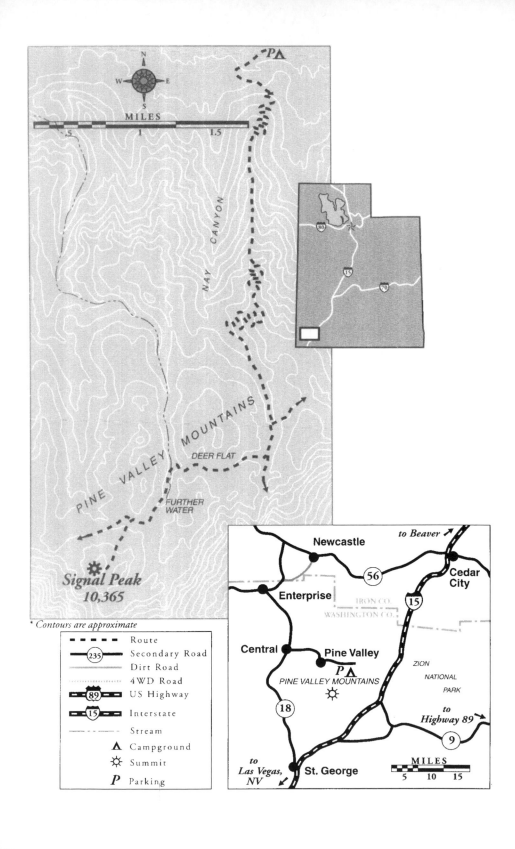

MILES

.5   1   1.5

P

NAY CANYON

PINE VALLEY MOUNTAINS

DEER FLAT

FURTHER WATER

Signal Peak
10,365

* *Contours are approximate*

- - - -   Route
235   Secondary Road
·········   Dirt Road
·········   4WD Road
89   US Highway
15   Interstate
- · - · -   Stream
▲   Campground
☼   Summit
P   Parking

to Beaver

Newcastle

Cedar City

56

15

Enterprise

IRON CO.
WASHINGTON CO.

Central

Pine Valley

P▲

PINE VALLEY MOUNTAINS

☼

ZION

NATIONAL

PARK

to Highway 89

18

9

to Las Vegas, NV

St. George

MILES

5   10   15

Signal Peak
10,365 feet
Washington County

Time:  7.5–8.5 hours   4–5.5 hours

Distance: 13 miles

Difficulty: Difficult

Starting Elevation: 6,880 feet

Elevation Gain: 3,485 feet

USGS Map: Signal Peak

➤ Trailhead
• From Cedar City, take Utah Highway 56 west about 30 miles to Newcastle.
• Turn left/southwest and drive about 9 miles to Utah 18 near Enterprise.
• Turn left/south on Utah Highway 18 and drive 18 miles to Central.
• Turn left/east and head to Pine Valley, about 8 miles.
• Turn left at the Pine Valley Church and drive 2 to 3 miles into the campground. Look for the signs leading to the Brown's Point Trail trailhead.

➤ Camping
There are three campgrounds near the trailhead: Juniper Park, Blue Springs, and Pines. They each have drinking water and restroom facilities, and each charges a fee.

➤ Tips and Precautions
The beginning of this hike can be very hot. Get started early in the morning before the temperatures start baking the lower part of the trail. Be sure to carry extra water.

ENGELMANN SPRUCE

Crossing the upper meadow with Signal Peak in the background

> The Hike

There are 151 miles of trails running throughout the Pine Valley
Mountains, northeast of St. George. The Brown's Point Trail leaves from a cul-
de-sac in one of the campgrounds and gently climbs more than 3 miles up and
over a ridge, then it drops into the densely forested Nay Canyon. At the 4-mile
point, near the head of Nay Canyon, the trail reaches a junction with the
Summit Trail, which stretches 35 miles across the ridge of the range. Elevations
range from 6,000 feet to 10,365 feet—Signal Peak.

From the junction, take a right and continue south, following the trail leading to an intersection with Oak Grove Trail. At that junction, about half a
mile, turn right/west and follow the sign to Further Water.

The trail climbs and then crosses a lush Alpine meadow. After the meadow,
the trail climbs again gently through the forest to a saddle that's not very obvious to hikers. The trail then bends to the left and heads downhill along rocky
terrain. At the bottom, the trail comes to the edge of a meadow. Cross the
stream and turn left/south, hiking across the meadow. You can see Signal Peak
straight ahead. The trail goes back into some trees as it traverses the mountain.
After about 100 to 150 yards, turn left off the trail and find a route toward the
summit in an obvious gully.

Stay on the right side of this drainage. Near the top, there are two distinct
knobs forming summits. Angle right/west away from the drainage to the small
summit plateau on the right. Move west across the top until you can see the
spectacular view on the other side. The peak is among the rocks where you
might find a cairn.

> Background

Legend has it that Signal Peak was named during World War II when bea-
cons were placed on the mountain to guide airplanes at night. The range was
likely named for its abundance of pine trees, which served the first sawmills
that were built there in 1855–56.

The Forest Service aptly calls the range "a mountain island surrounded by
desert."

> For More Information
  • Dixie National Forest, Pine Valley Ranger District, 196 E. Tabernacle,
  St. George, UT 84770, (435) 673-3431.
  • *Hiking Utah*, by Dave Hall, Falcon, 1997.

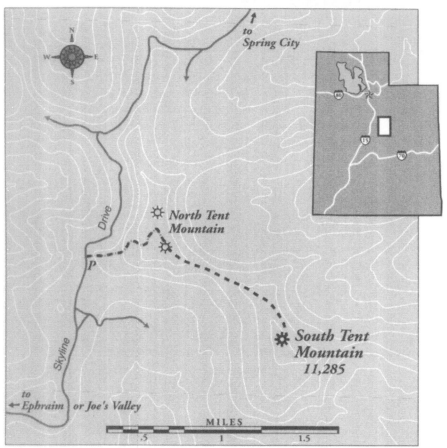

to
Spring City

North Tent
Mountain

P

Drive

Skyline

South Tent
Mountain
11,285

to
←Ephraim or Joe's Valley

MILES

.5   1   1.5

* Contours are approximate

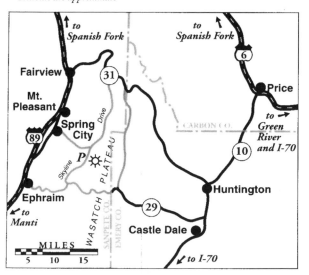

to
Spanish Fork

to
Spanish Fork

6

Fairview

31

Price

Mt.
Pleasant

Drive

Spring
City

89

CARBON CO.

to
Green
River
and I-70

P

10

WASATCH PLATEAU

Ephraim

Skyline

29

Huntington

to
Manti

Castle Dale

MILES

5   10   15

SANPETE CO.
EMERY CO.

to I-70

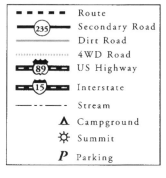

	Route
235	Secondary Road
	Dirt Road
	4WD Road
89	US Highway
15	Interstate
	Stream
▲	Campground
☼	Summit
P	Parking

South Tent Mountain*
11,285 feet
Sanpete County

Time:　🐢　2–2.5 hours　🐇　1–1.5 hours

Distance: 3 miles

Difficulty: Easy

Starting Elevation: 10,522 feet

Elevation Gain: 763 feet

USGS Maps: Spring City and South Tent Mountain

➤ Trailhead
• In Spring City, turn east at a sign pointing to Spring City Canyon.
• The road surface is dirt after leaving town. Drive three miles from the turnoff to a Y intersection. Stay left.
• This road reaches another intersection in 2.8 miles, which branches right to the Spring City picnic area. Stay left on the main road.
• The road climbs 7.2 miles up onto the Wasatch Plateau. Turn right onto Skyline Drive, which runs across the top of the plateau.
• Drive 3.3 miles to a sign that reads "South Tent Mountain."
• A road turns left here and heads to the top of North Tent Mountain. But it's probably better to park here and make the rest of the trip on foot because the road is badly rutted and eroded.

➤ Camping
There are no improved campgrounds near the trailhead. Restrooms and drinking water are available at the Spring City picnic area.

➤ Tips and Precautions
This hike can be combined with Carbon County's Monument Peak and Emery County's East Mountain in one weekend or possibly one day. But we recommend spending time at each area because each of the three peaks is surrounded by beautiful camping and recreation areas that should be enjoyed and explored.
The roads leading to South Tent Mountain can become slick and dangerous when they are wet.

*See the background information about Monument Peak (page 69), showing how hikes for East Mountain, Monument Peak, and South Tent Mountain can be combined into one trip.

MIKE EDGES HIS WAY ALONG THE EAST SIDE OF THE RIDGE

SOUTH TENT MOUNTAIN IN THE DISTANCE

➤ The Hike

Hike up along the dirt road to the top of North Tent Mountain. Then follow animal trails right/southeast down the saddle and up the left/northeast side of South Tent Mountain. The summit is surrounded by survey markers.

This is an easy and enjoyable hike. From the top, you can see many of Utah's county high peaks, including nearby East Mountain to the northeast, on the other side of Joes Valley.

➤ Background

Both North Tent and South Tent mountains probably got their names from the way they resemble old-fashioned, A-shaped tents.

➤ For More Information

• Manti-La Sal National Forest, Sanpete Ranger District, 150 S. Main St., Ephraim, UT 84627, (435) 283-4151.

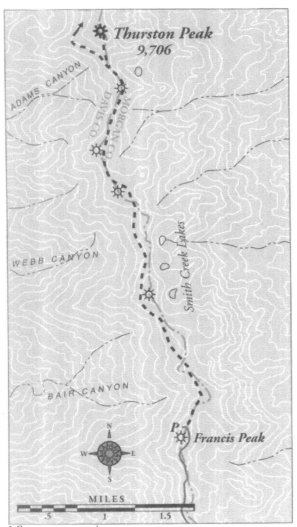

Thurston Peak
9,706

ADAMS CANYON

MORGAN CO.

DAVIS CO.

WEBB CANYON

Smith Creek Lakes

BAIR CANYON

N
W E
S

P
Francis Peak

MILES

.5   1   1.5

* Contours are approximate

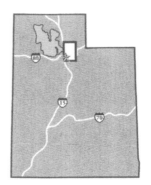

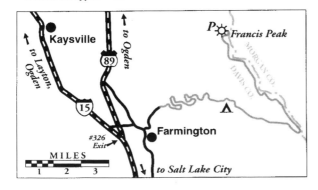

Kaysville

to Ogden

to Layton, Ogden

to Ogden

P
Francis Peak

MORGAN CO.

DAVIS CO.

89

15

#326
Exit

Farmington

MILES

1   2   3

to Salt Lake City

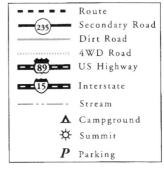

▬ ▬ ▬ ▬	Route
▬▬(235)▬▬	Secondary Road
▬▬▬▬	Dirt Road
··············	4WD Road
▬(89)▬	US Highway
▬(15)▬	Interstate
— - — - —	Stream
▲	Campground
☼	Summit
P	Parking

Thurston Peak
9,706 feet
Davis and Morgan Counties

Time:  5–6 hours 3.5–4 hours
Distance: 8 miles
Difficulty: Easy
Starting Elevation: 9,265 feet
Elevation Gain: 441 feet
USGS Map: Peterson

➤ Trailhead
• From the south on Interstate 15, take Exit 326 for U.S. Highway 89/South Ogden. Immediately turn off Highway 89 at Exit 327 for Lagoon Drive/Farmington. (From the north on Interstate 15, take Exit 327 for Lagoon Drive/Farmington.)
• Turn right onto U.S. Highway 106, which is Farmington's Main Street.
• Turn left onto 600 North, which is a scenic backway.
• Turn left on 100 East, which climbs into Farmington Canyon.
• After 8 miles, you'll reach a junction. Drive through the left gate and follow the road to the radar installation atop Francis Peak. Park here; the trail follows the ridgeline to the north.

➤ Camping
Sunset Campground is located 5.3 miles up Farmington Canyon after you turn onto 100 East. It has restroom facilities, but no drinking water. There is no fee.

➤ Tips and Precautions
The drive to the top of Francis Peak is certainly not for the faint of heart. The narrow road winds up the mountain, with steep dropoffs from the side of the roadway. As you approach the radar facility, there may be little room on the road for oncoming vehicles to pass each other.

LEAVING FRANCIS PEAK

DIANE AND MIKE GLISSADE FROM THE RIDGE

➤ The Hike

Most of the elevation climbed on this hike is done in your car, but that shouldn't discourage avid outdoors people. The 4-mile hike from Francis to Thurston provides spectacular views of the Great Salt Lake on one side and Morgan Valley on the other.

The first half of the trail follows a maintenance road north from the radar facility across the top of the ridge. A trail continues along the ridge to Thurston Peak, which is marked by a plaque telling the story of its namesake.

The hike is relatively easy and climbs up and down a handful of minor peaks along the ridge. It takes roughly the same amount of time to hike to Thurston Peak as it does to hike back.

DIANE AND MIKE TRAVERSE A STEEP SNOWFIELD IN THE EARLY SPRING

MARK ELEZY RETURNS FROM THURSTON, WHICH RISES IN THE BACKGROUND

MIKE DOES A BALANCING ACT ACROSS A SNOWFIELD

➤ Background

Older maps and guidebooks refer to the peak as North Francis Peak for its proximity to Francis Peak, which was named after a pioneer woman who helped early surveyors in the region. Thurston Peak was renamed in 1993 for Mormon pioneer Thomas Jefferson Thurston, who moved into the Morgan Valley below these mountains in 1852. He is credited for blazing a road through Weber Canyon.

The trail to Thurston Peak follows a portion of the Great Western Trail. The GWT is a north-south corridor of trails and passageways running from Canada to Mexico, through Arizona, Utah, Wyoming, Idaho, and Montana. Until recently, it was only a concept, but now, land management agencies have installed GWT signs on many of the individual routes that are a part of the interstate trail.

➤ For More Information

• Wasatch-Cache National Forest, Salt Lake Ranger District, 6944 S. 3000 East, Salt Lake City, UT 84121, (801) 943-1794.

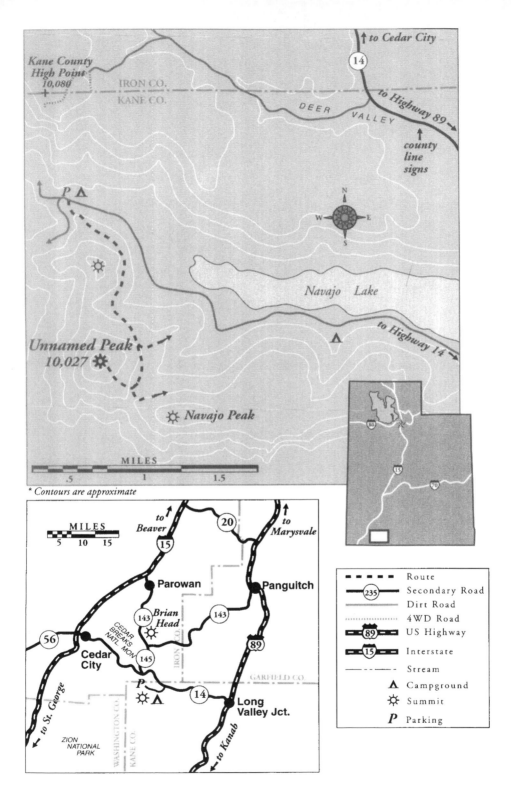

Unnamed Peak*

10,027 feet
Kane County

Time: 🐢 2–3 hours   🐇 1.5–1.75 hours

Distance: 3.5 miles

Difficulty: Easy

Starting Elevation: 9,160 feet

Elevation Gain: 867 feet

USGS Map: Navajo Lake

➤ Trailhead
• From Cedar City, drive east on Utah Highway 14 up Cedar Canyon.
(Another option, if coming from the north, is to turn off at Parowan and take
Utah Highway 143. This highway links up with Utah 14 after passing through
Cedar Breaks National Monument.)
• Take the Navajo Lake turnoff, 26 miles from Cedar City (8 miles beyond
Utah Highway 143).
• Follow the road around to the southern side of the lake and continue to
Te-ah Campground at the southwest end. Stay on the paved road with the
campground on your right until the pavement ends at a junction with a gravel
road on the left. Park here.
• Walk back along the paved road about 50 yards to the trailhead, on the south
side of the road.

➤ Camping
   The Te-ah Campground has drinking water and restroom facilities, and it
charges a fee.

➤ Tips and Precautions
   The last section of the route climbs off the trail where route-finding is necessary for this rarely climbed mountain. Pay specific attention, so you can
retrace your route back. If you stray too far south while hiking off the peak,
you will likely drop below the saddle and into a gully. Route-finding from this
gully is difficult because landmarks are obscured by the trees.

*When *The Salt Lake Tribune* started running a series of stories in 1996 about Utah's county
high peaks, it also ran a contest to name the three peaks that were unnamed. The winner for

► The Hike

Kane County is unusual in that its highest peak is not the county's highest point. The highest point is actually the side of a mountain with a peak in nearby Iron County. (A similar situation can be found in Wasatch County.) Fortunately, the highest point and highest peak surround Navajo Lake.

For the highest peak, follow the Virgin River Rim Trail south from the road next to Te-ah Campground. After about 1 to 1.5 miles, the trail meets the Lodge Trail, which drops down to the east. Continue on the Virgin River Rim Trail for another 0.5 mile or so, where it reaches a saddle between Navajo Peak and the unnamed county high peak. The highest peak in Kane County is on the right. Hike off the trail and find a route to the top.

MIKE CHECKS OUT A BRISTLECONE PINE

The highest point in Kane County can be seen just to the left of the cliff band across the lakebed to the north. A dirt road leads to the high point.

Drive back up Utah Highway 14 to the border between Kane and Iron counties. Turn west on Forest Service Road 0055, which heads to Deer Valley. On the USGS topographic map, the turnoff for this road is just below the county line in Kane County, but signs along the highway put it just above the county line in Iron County. Continue down this road to Forest Service Road 1642 and turn left. Drive to the intersection of Forest Service Road 1647. Most people will want to park here and continue walking up Road 1642 until it ends. But a good 4-wheel-drive vehicle with high clearance may be able to drive to the end of the road.

From here, wander uphill to the southwest toward the cliffs. This is roughly the highest point in Kane County.

Kane County was Andrew "Andy" Nelson Peak. Nelson apparently made his life work surveying in the county. At the time of this writing, the Utah Geological Survey had yet to adopt the names.

THE SUMMIT IS A FLAT MEADOW

➤ Background

The highest peak is reached from the Virgin River Rim Trail, a relatively new scenic trail for hikers, mountain bikers, and horseback riders that was built by volunteers and the Forest Service.

Some of the oldest trees in the world, bristlecone pines, are found all around this peak.

Navajo Lake, named following a skirmish near the lake between stockmen and Indians, drains through volcanic lava tubes that are partly responsible for nearby Cascade Falls, south of the lake.

➤ For More Information

• Dixie National Forest, Cedar City Ranger District, 82 N. 100 East, Cedar City, UT 84721, (435) 865-3200.

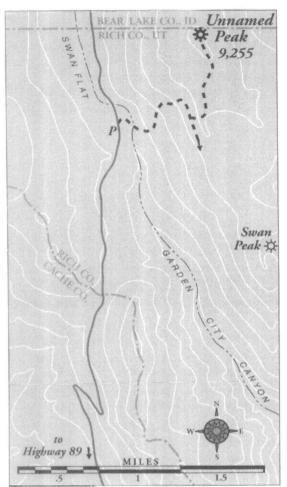

Unnamed
Peak
9,255

SWAN FLAT

P

RICH CO.
CACHE CO.

GARDEN CITY CANYON

Swan
Peak ☼

to
Highway 89 ↓

MILES

.5   1   1.5

* Contours are approximate

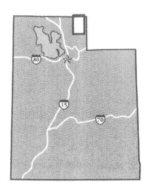

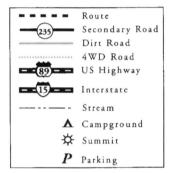

▬ ▬ ▬	Route
═(235)═	Secondary Road
───────	Dirt Road
··········	4WD Road
▬(89)▬	US Highway
▬(15)▬	Interstate
─·─·─	Stream
▲	Campground
☼	Summit
P	Parking

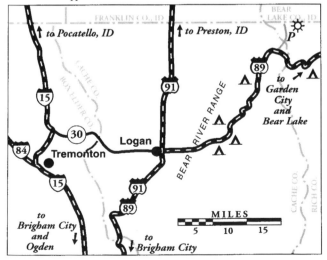

↑ to Pocatello, ID   ↑ to Preston, ID   ☼
                                                        P

CACHE CO.
BOX ELDER CO.

(15)

(91)

(89)

to
Garden
City
and
Bear Lake

(30)   Logan   BEAR RIVER RANGE

(84)   Tremonton

(15)   (91)

                        (89)

CACHE CO.
RICH CO.

to
Brigham City
and
Ogden ↓

to
↓ Brigham City

MILES

5   10   15

Unnamed Peak*

9,255 feet
Rich County

Time: 🐢 1.25–2 hours 🐇 0.5–1 hour

Distance: 3 miles

Difficulty: Easy

Starting Elevation: 8,322 feet

Elevation Gain: 933 feet

USGS Map: Garden City

➤ Trailhead
• From 400 North (U.S. Highway 89) in Logan, drive east to Logan Canyon. After you drive past Utah State University and drop down a hill, the highway crosses Logan River before climbing into the canyon.
• After crossing the bridge, drive 28.5 miles up Logan Canyon. (3.1 miles after the Beaver Mountain ski area turnoff.)
• Shortly after passing the Utah Department of Transportation maintenance shed, turn left/north onto Swan Flat Road.
• Drive about 3.5 miles up this dirt road. It switchbacks twice, climbing up to a pass, and continues north. Keep an eye out to the right/east. The road reaches a clearing where Garden City Canyon drops off to the right. Park here. An ATV trail connects with the road at this point. If you miss the trailhead, you'll know it when the relatively flat road starts down a gentle grade.

➤ Camping
The nearest campgrounds to the trailhead are Lewis M. Turner at the Tony Grove Lake turnoff and Sunrise, beyond the Swan Flat Road turnoff. Both have drinking water and restroom facilities. Sunrise charges a fee.

➤ Tips and precautions
When you leave the ATV trail, head north. The forest is dense and landmarks are not easy to see.

*When *The Salt Lake Tribune* started running a series of stories in 1996 about Utah's county high peaks, it also ran a contest to name the three peaks that were unnamed. The winner for Rich County was Bridger Peak, named after mountain man and trapper Jim Bridger, who spent much of his life in the area. At the time of this writing, the Utah Geological Survey had yet to adopt the name.

Diane Bush climbs the steep ATV trail

A LARGE DEAD TREE IS A LANDMARK FOR THE HIGHEST POINT

➤ The Hike

Follow the ATV trail as it heads down, east across the top of Garden City Canyon. This trail then climbs the steep hillside, almost to the ridgeline between Swan Peak on the right/south and the unnamed county high peak on the left/north. But you won't see either of these landmarks.

When the ATV trail turns and heads right/south to Swan Peak, continue down the trail just a short way. Get off the trail and head left/north of the cliff bands that run to the south. You might have to wander around a bit, looking for the highest spot. In 1997, a large dead tree helped mark the highest peak.

➤ Background

From Rich County's highest peak, you can look out over the turquoise waters of Bear Lake on the east. This lake straddles the Utah-Idaho border and is a popular destination for fishing, boating, and jet-skiing.

➤ For More Information

• Wasatch-Cache National Forest, Logan Ranger District, 1500 E. Highway 89, Logan, UT 84321, (435) 755-3620.

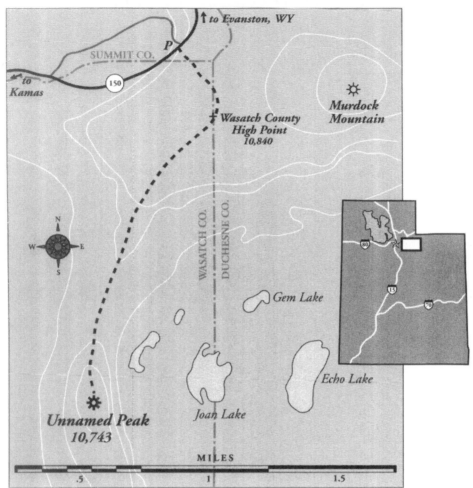

↑ to Evanston, WY

P

SUMMIT CO.

150

to
Kamas

✝ Wasatch County
High Point
10,840

☼
Murdock
Mountain

WASATCH CO.

DUCHESNE CO.

Gem Lake

Echo Lake

☼
Unnamed Peak
10,743

Joan Lake

MILES

.5   1   1.5

* Contours are approximate

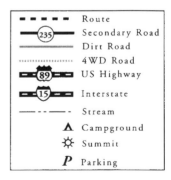

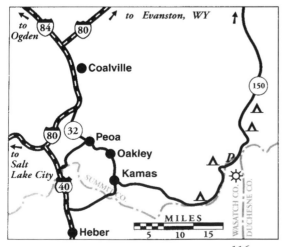

to Evanston, WY ↑

84   80

to
Ogden

● Coalville

150

▲

▲

80   32

● Peoa

● Oakley

▲   P

to
Salt
Lake City

● Kamas

40

SUMMIT CO.

☼

▲

WASATCH CO.

DUCHESNE CO.

● Heber

MILES

5   10   15

Legend:

- - - - Route
━ 235 ━ Secondary Road
━━━━ Dirt Road
········· 4WD Road
━ 89 ━ US Highway
━ 15 ━ Interstate
—·—·— Stream
▲ Campground
☼ Summit
P Parking

116

Unnamed Peak*

10,743 feet
Wasatch County

Time:  1.75–2 hours   1–1.25 hours

Distance: 3 miles

Difficulty: Easy

Starting Elevation: 10,587 feet

Elevation Gain: 156 feet

USGS Map: Mirror Lake

➤ Trailhead
• From Kamas, drive east on Utah Highway 150 (the Mirror Lake Highway).
• Park at mile marker 28. There's a turnout for parking on the north side of the highway.

➤ Camping
There are numerous campgrounds along the Mirror Lake Highway. The closest one to the trailhead is probably Lost Lake (Lost Creek in some publications). All of the Forest Service campgrounds along this highway have drinking water and restroom facilities, and all of them charge a fee.

➤ Tips and Precautions
There is no trail. The high peak is marked by a giant cairn, but locating the high point is likely to be just a good guess. We recommend a map and compass.

*When *The Salt Lake Tribune* started running a series of stories in 1996 about Utah's county high peaks, it also ran a contest to name the three peaks that were unnamed. The winner for Wasatch County was Mount Cardwell. Henry Cardwell Clegg, a lifelong resident of Wasatch County, spent 56 years developing and maintaining water and recreation near this peak.

GETTING A COMPASS BEARING

DIANE BUSH NEAR THE COUNTY'S HIGH POINT. THE HIGH PEAK IS IN THE BACKGROUND.

> The Hike

Wasatch County, like Kane County, is unusual in that its highest peak is not its highest point. The highest point is on the side of Murdock Mountain, whose summit is in adjacent Duchesne County. Fortunately, the high peak and high point can be reached in the same hike.

From the parking turnout, cross the highway south. You may want to check your compass and chose a southeast heading that will first take you to the top of the highest point. Route-finding can be particularly tricky in the dense forest leading to the high point.

After reaching what is likely the highest point in the county, look south. You can see the highest peak from this point. Hike downhill and across a relatively flat area characterized by rocky fields before climbing up to the boulder-strewn summit.

MIKE WAVES FROM THE TOP

> Background

Starting in 1997, motorists were obliged to pay a toll on the Mirror Lake Highway if they planned to stop anywhere along it. The highway is a popular scenic byway, providing access to high mountain lakes and scenic viewpoints like the Slate Gorge overlook, Provo River Falls, and the Bald Mountain overlook.

The Uinta Mountains are one of two major ranges in the United States that run east-west rather than north-south; the Brooks range in Alaska is the other. The Uintas are also home to several of the highest mountains in Utah, including the state's highest, Kings Peak.

> For More Information

• Wasatch-Cache National Forest, Kamas Ranger District, 50 E. Center St., Kamas, UT 84036, (435) 783-4338.

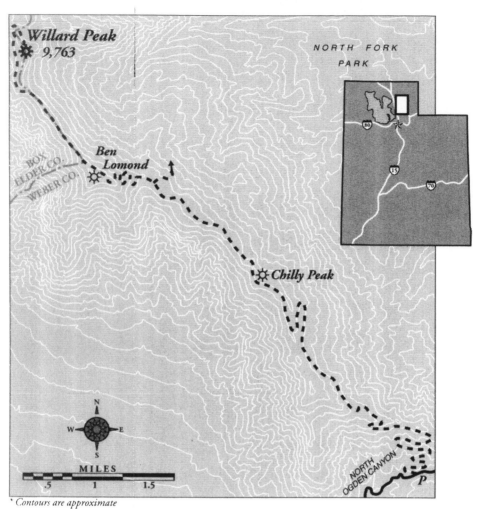

Willard Peak
9,763

NORTH FORK
PARK

BOX ELDER CO.
WEBER CO.

Ben Lomond

✲*Chilly Peak*

N
W E
S

MILES
.5   1   1.5

NORTH OGDEN CANYON

P

* *Contours are approximate*

BOX ELDER CO.
WEBER CO.

to I-15
and Brigham City

North
Ogden

3100 N.

Liberty

P

to
Pineview
Reservoir

1050 E.

134

235

to
I-15
and
Exit #352

Washington Blvd.

2600 N.

89

Ogden

MILES
1   2   3

▪ ▪ ▪ ▪	Route
〔235〕	Secondary Road
	Dirt Road
⋯⋯⋯	4WD Road
〔89〕	US Highway
〔15〕	Interstate
— ‥ —	Stream
▲	Campground
✲	Summit
P	Parking

Willard Peak

9,763 feet
Weber County

Time: 🐢 9–10 hours   🐇 7–8 hours

Distance: 19 miles

Difficulty: Difficult

Starting Elevation: 6,180 feet

Elevation Gain: 3,583 feet

USGS Maps: North Ogden and Mantua

➤ Trailhead
• From Interstate 15, take Exit 352 for North Ogden/Farr West.
• Drive east on Utah Highway 134. At the traffic light, turn right onto U.S. Highway 89.
• Turn left/east onto Utah Highway 235. Turn left/north onto Washington Blvd.
• Drive north into North Ogden and turn right/east on 2600 North.
• Turn left/north on 1050 East.
• Turn right/east on 3100 North, which leads into North Ogden Canyon. The trailhead is located at the pass, where the road starts to drop into Ogden Valley. There are restrooms located at the spacious parking lot on the south side of the road. The well-marked trail starts directly across the road, north of the parking lot.

➤ Camping
   North Fork Park Campground is over the pass in Ogden Valley, north of Liberty.

➤ Tips and Precautions
   The beginning of this hike is on an extreme south exposure and even though the switchbacks are not steep, heat exhaustion can be a very real problem on an average warm day. Start early and bring plenty of water.
   This is a very long hike. Don't pay attention to the mileage listed on trail signs, because the signs contradict one another. Ben Lomond is approximately 8.1 miles from the trailhead; Willard is about 1.4 miles farther.

► The Hike

The hike itself is relatively easy, except for the distance, which makes for a very long day. The trail has three distinct sections: the switchbacks, the ridge, and the climb.

The trail starts at the summit of North Ogden Canyon. Several gentle switchbacks make the climb easy, but keep in mind that the return trip later in the day will take a while because much of it is simply going back and forth down the switches.

Scrub oak and mountain mahogany cover the hillsides, which are open to a hot southern exposure along the switchbacks. Once you round the top of the ridge, tall evergreens provide a shady break. During this section of the climb, the trail stretches below the east side of the ridge leading to Ben Lomond.

PHOTO BY DIANE BUSH

DAN PLAYING AROUND ON BEN LOMOND

It's a leisurely stroll along the ridge, which crosses to the west side after about a mile and a half. On the west side, you get your first spectacular glimpse of both Ben Lomond and Willard Peak, rising high above the valley floor along steep and exposed cliffs.

There is a sign at Baily Springs trail junction, where the trail meets the base of Ben Lomond. The climbing starts here. The well-trodden path turns rocky as it climbs short switchbacks up Ben Lomond. The steep climbing is worth the effort once you reach the top, where a plaque describes the mountain and the city below it. From here, you'll drop north down to the saddle between Ben Lomond and Willard. The trail wraps around the west side of Willard and climbs up to the peak's northern ridge.

To this point, the trail is well established, but the last 0.25-mile hike south to Willard's summit is mostly through rocks, brush, and scree, with only occasional sections of a trail visible. Several survey markers highlight the flat-topped summit.

MARK ELZEY WITH WILLARD PEAK IN THE BACKGROUND

LOOKING DOWN AT WILLARD BAY FROM WILLARD PEAK

➤ Background

Climbing Willard is simply climbing its more popular neighbor Ben Lomond, and then some. Willard is 47 feet higher, but Ben Lomond is more prominent in the Ogden skyline. In fact, the lower peak, named after a similar mountain in the Scottish highlands, was the inspiration for the Paramount Pictures logo.

Willard was named after the town at its base, midway between Ogden and Brigham City. Both were named to honor Willard Richards, a counselor to Mormon Church leader Brigham Young.

From the summits of Willard and Ben Lomond, you can look west down steep and rugged quartzite cliffs and out to the vast Great Salt Lake. From

DIANE BUSH CLIMBS THE NORTH SHOULDER

Willard's north ridge, you can see a road that was built in 1936 by the Civilian Conservation Corps. Peak baggers looking for an easy climb of Willard can drive this road up from Mantua. It passes within half a mile of the peak, on its way through Willard Basin to the top of nearby Inspiration Point.

➤ For More Information
• Wasatch-Cache National Forest, Ogden Ranger District, 507 25th St., Suite 103, Ogden, UT 84401, (801) 625-5112.

Utah Classics

When we started this project in 1996, it was quite obvious that a book about just the county high peaks wouldn't be enough, as some of the most prominent mountains in Utah are not the tallest in their counties.

Mount Timpanogos, for example, has been described as the most prominent mountain along the 200-mile length of the Wasatch range. It has been used as a training ground by climbers headed to Everest. But it's still 179 feet shorter than Utah County's highest peak, Mount Nebo.

We also chose to highlight the Wellsville Cone, which isn't even the highest peak in the Wellsville Mountains. But people in northern Utah can't deny its appeal.

Olympus not only towers over Salt Lake City, its name conjures up images of mighty gods. How could this be left out of a guidebook featuring Utah's mountains?

We also picked Notch Peak. You won't find it on many postcards. In fact, Notch Peak is tucked away in the state's remote western desert. But a few people know that, in terms of big wall climbing, Notch Peak is only a few feet shorter than Yosemite's famous Half Dome. People who aren't interested in rock climbing, however, can easily hike to its summit.

Our choices were quite subjective and biased after hiking in each of the state's twenty-nine counties in the summer of 1997. We could have certainly chosen more "classic" peaks to highlight, but a line had to be drawn somewhere. We believe all four classics in this book provide enjoyable hikes, worthy of being counted among the state's top peaks.

Looking for a change of pace, photographer Dan Miller took a notepad along on these four hikes while co-author Mike Weibel stayed at home compiling notes from the previous twenty-six mountains. Dan authored the following four chapters, which Mike later helped edit.

Dan estimated the times for the tortoise icon based on his past hiking experiences with Mike. He also managed to shoot pictures of himself when no one else was accompanying him.

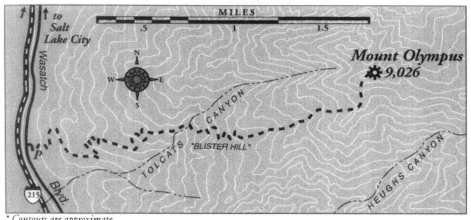

* *Contours are approximate*

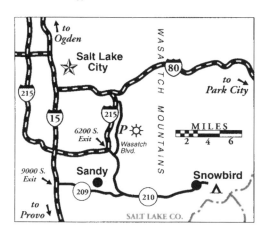

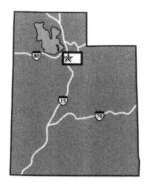

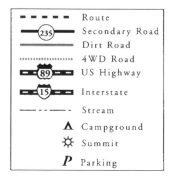

- - - - -	Route
═235═	Secondary Road
──────	Dirt Road
··············	4WD Road
═89═	US Highway
═15═	Interstate
─ · ─ · ─	Stream
▲	Campground
☼	Summit
P	Parking

Mount Olympus
9,026 feet

Time:  6–7 hours ⟶ 4–5 hours

Distance: 7.5 miles

Difficulty: Difficult

Starting Elevation: 4,880 feet

Elevation Gain: 4,146 feet

USGS Map: Sugarhouse

➤ Trailhead
• Take the 6200 South exit from Interstate 215 on the east side of the Salt Lake Valley.
• Drive east on Utah Highway 210 and make a left turn onto Wasatch Boulevard. It is about 1.5 miles to the small parking lot on the right/east side of the highway by "Pete's Rock."

➤ Camping*
There are no improved camp-grounds near the trailhead.

➤ Tips and Precautions
Mid-season is probably not a good time to attempt this hike because of the heat at the lower elevation. The sun can be unrelenting. Bring lots of water, and watch for rattlesnakes, which are known to be abundant.

There is a bit of precarious scram-bling in the last 600 feet before the summit, but it's not badly exposed unless you get off the route.

*Although there are no improved camp-grounds near the trailhead, try finding one in nearby Little Cottonwood Canyon. See the camping information for American Fork Twin Peaks.

THE LAST SECTION OF TRAIL

➤ The Hike

The trail starts just south of a local rock-climbing area called "Pete's Rock," on the east side of Wasatch Boulevard. It begins by climbing north, up several steep erosion-control steps, to a point just above "Pete's Rock." It then switchbacks to the right/east and connects with an old fading trail coming up from the right/southeast and Tolcats Canyon.

The trail makes a left/north turn here, then makes several switchbacks through juniper and sage, opening to views across the Salt Lake Valley. Eventually, it runs back into a wooded area of Tolcats Canyon, where you reach a small stream crossing. Don't follow the water upstream. The trail crosses the stream.

DIANE BUSH ON THE LOWER TRAIL

The trail starts up the infamous 0.5-mile "Blister Hill," which now has switchbacks instead of its original "shortest distance between two points" route. After reaching a brief level section, enter the wooded steep gully. The trail follows the right edge of the gully and climbs steeply to the saddle.

The Olympus ridge defines the west wall of the gully and another impressive rock ridge walls in the east side. After another 0.5 mile, the east ridge fades out into the saddle. Follow the trail to the right and an incredible view of Hueghs Canyon, Big Cottonwood Canyon, and, in the distance, the awesome Twin Peaks.

From the saddle, turn to the left/northwest and enter a boulder-ridden gully that leads up 600 feet to the summit. Pay attention to the route for the descent. Once you make the ridge, the summit is 200 feet to the right/east.

Mount Olympus is actually two summits divided by a large gully. The summit that is visible from Salt Lake City is the front/north summit. The trail ends on the other, higher summit.

➤ Background

Mount Olympus is a Salt Lake City icon that graces the Wasatch ridgeline with its rugged-looking north face. Only minutes from downtown Salt Lake City, Mount Olympus is in a federally designated wilderness area.

PHOTO BY DIANE BUSH

DAN SCRAMBLING TO THE SUMMIT

DIANE BUSH SCRAMBLES UP THE LAST 600 FEET

Mount Olympus was named after the mythical home of gods in Greece.

Harold Goodro, a Wasatch Mountain legend, used the trail to Mount Olympus to train for his outdoor adventures. Goodro would load his pack with rocks from the trailhead and carry them to a spot just before the stream crossing, dump them, and return with a lighter pack to save his knees on the descent. This rock pile is still there.

The trailhead is located just south of "Pete's Rock," a large rock outcropping along Wasatch Boulevard that has been a part of Salt Lake climbing history. Goodro nicknamed the rock after O'Dell Peterson, who was the main inspiration for climbers in the 1930s. The rock is used by beginning climbers as well as more experienced climbers who want to hone their skills and techniques.

ON THE SUMMIT

➤ For More Information
• Wasatch-Cache National Forest, Salt Lake Ranger District, 6944 S. 3000 East, Salt Lake City, UT 84121, (801) 943-1794.
• *Hiking the Wasatch*, by John Veranth, Wasatch Mountain Club, 1988.
• *Trails of The Wasatch, A Pocket Guide*, by Gary C. Nichols, Nichols, 1996

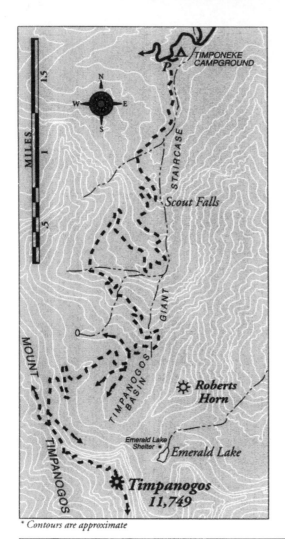

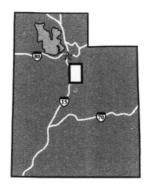

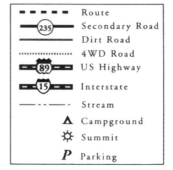

▬ ▬ ▬ ▬	Route
━235━	Secondary Road
━━━	Dirt Road
┈┈┈┈	4WD Road
━89━	US Highway
━15━	Interstate
━·━·━	Stream
▲	Campground
☼	Summit
P	Parking

* *Contours are approximate*

Mount Timpanogos
11,749 feet

Time: 🐢 9–11 hours 🐇 5.5–6.5 hours

Distance: 14 miles

Difficulty: Extreme

Starting Elevation: 7,360 feet

Elevation Gain: 4,389 feet

USGS Map: Timpanogos Cave

➤ Trailhead

• From Interstate 15, take Exit 287 for Highland and Alpine.

• Turn east onto Utah Highway 92. In 8 miles you will enter American Fork Canyon and pass a toll booth.

• Continue along the Alpine Loop Highway past Timpanogos Cave for another 8.2 miles and turn right/west into Timpooneke Campground. The trailhead is a parking area on the left/south side of the road.

(From Provo Canyon via Heber or Provo, turn north on the Alpine Loop Highway. Pass the Sundance Ski Resort and continue to the Timpooneke Campground and turn left/west.)

➤ Camping

Timpooneke Campground has drinking water and restroom facilities. A fee is charged and reservations are recommended.

➤ Tips and Precautions

Have cash with you; there is an entrance fee for the Alpine Loop Highway.

Be aware that the hike is very long and the upper switchbacks are narrow, above steep scree slopes. There can be snow on the upper parts of the trail even in late summer, which can make the hike quite treacherous.

We advise against using the Aspen Grove route for the return descent. That route ascends the ridge to the summit from the south. There can be a large cornice above the snowfield that needs to be descended on that route. Several people have been seriously injured falling through the snow onto the jagged rocks underneath.

DAN DESCENDS THE UPPER SECTION OF THE TRAIL

► The Hike

There are two routes to the summit, Aspen Grove and Timpooneke. Even though it is slightly longer, we've picked the Timpooneke trail as our classic route. The gradual climb and the trail's reputation as one of the most spectacular trails in the area adds to this classic hiking experience.

Leaving the parking lot headed south, you will pass a bulletin board warning of fines for hikers who cut switchbacks. The gutted shortcuts running between the switches in the trail are one of the obvious signs of heavy use and abuse in the area.

After about 0.5 mile, the trail breaks through the trees and you can look south up at the "Giant Staircase" and the individual plateaus that form this tiered drainage. The trail begins its climb at this point, angling right/southwest along and above the meadow.

After another 1.5 miles, the trail breaks onto one of the terraces and makes a sharp turn back and to the right/north to follow the contour. After 0.5 mile, it turns back to the left/south again and continues up the route. At this point, the trail climbs through the upper and steeper portion of the "Giant Staircase." The terrain is more rugged and the views north toward the Salt Lake area Wasatch Mountains begin to grow more immense. American Fork Twin Peaks, the high summit for Salt Lake County, can be seen among its high neighbors like the 11,326-foot Pfeifferhorn.

The trail eventually tops out and enters Timpanogos Basin. Across the basin looms the massive 1,629-foot north face of Mount Timpanogos.

THE NORTH FACE OF MOUNT TIMPANOGOS

The Aspen Grove trail intersects here in the basin and continues up and over the pass to the Emerald Lake Shelter. Instead, you should stay right/west at the intersection and continue a short distance before making a switchback to the right/north. The trail will gradually angle back again to the left/west. The trail heads toward the headwall of the Timpanogos Basin and then makes long switchbacks up the steep wall to the saddle. The cities of Provo and Orem are tiny specks far below.

The summit is a little more than a 0.5-mile, 700-foot climb farther. The trail continues south on the right/west side of the ridge. The trail climbs through a tight slot between two rock walls making short switches. Do not continue on the false trail around the bottom of the south rock wall. The trail can get narrow above steep scree slopes, and extreme caution is advised if there is any snow or ice at this point.

The summit area is described in Dave Hall's book *Hiking Utah:* "A small, open, metal, hut-like structure, built as a triangulation station for the county, dominates the summit block where dedicated hikers of the early 1920s danced at sunrise."

➤ Background

Nicknamed "Timp," this massive summit with its prominent exposed rocky features towers over Utah Valley. It is the second highest summit in the 200-mile Wasatch range. Only Mount Nebo is higher. Timp easily earns our num-

TIMPANOGOS BASIN AND NORTH TO THE WASATCH MOUNTAINS

ber one classic status on its own merits and because it is probably the best-known summit in the state.

Mount Timpanogos is actually the 7-mile crest rising 7,000 feet above the Utah Valley floor. The summit from the valley floor appears as a small point in the middle of the crest.

A team of 15 Utahns camped on Timp during the winter of 1989–90. Their 10-day winter ascent was a training exercise for Mount Everest. Former Salt Lake City Mayor Ted Wilson and KSL reporter Doug Miller participated in the exercise. Expedition leader Doug Hansen, from Orem, and four others made an unsuccessful attempt on Everest in 1992. They reached an elevation of 25,000 feet before returning.

THE SHELTER ATOP THE SUMMIT

➤ For More Information
• Uinta National Forest, 88 W. 100 North, Provo, UT 84601,
(801) 377-5780.
• *Hiking Utah*, by Dave Hall, Falcon, 1997.
• *Utah Valley Trails*, by Shirley and Monroe Paxman and Gayle and
Weldon Taylor, Wasatch, 1978.
• *Climbing and Exploring Utah's Mt. Timpanogos*, by Michael Kelsey,
Kelsey Publishing Co., 1989.

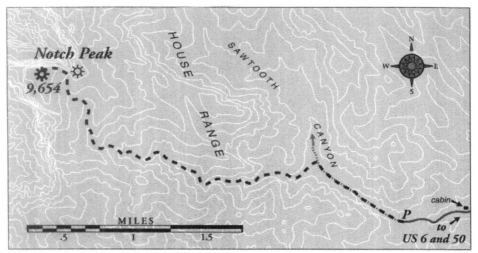

Contours are approximate

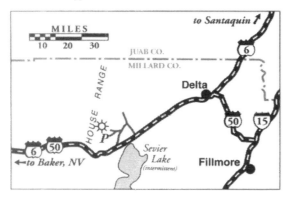

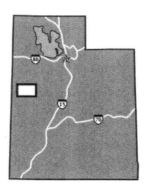

- - - - -	Route
━(235)━	Secondary Road
―――	Dirt Road
··············	4WD Road
━(89)━	US Highway
━(15)━	Interstate
— · — · —	Stream
▲	Campground
☼	Summit
P	Parking

Notch Peak

9,654 feet

A Utah Classic

Time: 🐢 4.5–5 hours 🐇 3–3.5 hours

Distance: 7.5 miles

Difficulty: Moderate

Starting Elevation: 6,860 feet

Elevation Gain: 2,794 feet

USGS Maps: Miller Cove and Notch Peak

➤ Trailhead

• From the town side of the bridge on the west side of Delta, drive west on U.S. Highway 50 for 41.5 miles. Turn right/north onto a dirt road.

• After 1 mile, a road joins this one on the left. Continue on the original road for another 2.4 miles and turn left/northwest on the road leading to Miller Canyon. In 1997, there was a sign facing northbound motorists indicating the direction to the canyon.

• After 5.3 miles, turn left/southwest toward Miller Cove. Then, after another 2.7 miles, you will see an old miner's cabin is on the right/north. Low-clearance vehicles might consider parking here. A little farther, 0.7 mile, the road drops into the streambed and becomes a 4-wheel-drive trail up a deeply cut canyon. Park here.

(If approaching from Nevada, drive 47.8 miles east of the border on U.S. Highway 50 and turn left/north on the dirt road.)

➤ Camping

There are no improved campgrounds in this area.

➤ Tips and Precautions

Watch carefully for the first left turn up the drainage leaving Sawtooth Canyon. As you approach the top of the drainage, it splits. Take the left fork. If there is debris, skirt around it on the right.

This is a good summit to hike in the early spring or late fall because of the lower elevation. With the dry Utah west desert, snow should not be a problem. Flash floods in the narrow wash can be a danger in late summer and early fall.

> The Hike

After parking, follow the 4-wheel-drive trail as it drops into the drainage and continue walking through Sawtooth Canyon. A beautiful cliff wall rises several hundred feet on the left/southwest side. After about 0.75 mile, watch for another drainage coming in from the left/southwest. Walk a little farther until the drainage merges with Sawtooth Canyon. Make a left/southwest turn up the drainage. There is no trail here, but the drainage is well defined. It narrows with steep canyon walls that make it feel like a southern Utah redrock canyon hike.

After 2 miles the wash becomes steeper with several rock ledges that need to be negotiated. It was in this area that a large tree was across the wash in 1997. Look just above this for one of the bristlecone pines.

THE NORTH FACE OF NOTCH PEAK

After another 0.5 mile the wash turns right/north and then splits. Look up and you will see Notch Peak to the left. Straight ahead and to the right of Notch Peak is a more defined peak. Your destination is the saddle between the two.

Take the left/west fork. If there is debris in the wash, navigate to the right/north hillside. The wash eventually disappears, leaving an easy shot to the saddle. After catching your breath from the spectacular view, head left/west up the steep slope to the Notch Peak summit.

> Background

Notch Peak is just that—a well-defined notch in the House Range of west-central Utah. The peak has the most impressive vertical drop in the state, which earned it our classic title.

Notch Peak's limestone north face drops a sheer 2,200 feet into the canyon below and towers 5,000 feet above the Tule Valley floor to the west.

Bristlecone pines, which are some of the oldest living trees on earth, make this area home. There are several along the route to the summit, and a large grove to the right of the saddle. They are worth a side trip before descending.

142

DIANE BUSH LOOKS OVER THE EDGE

➤ For More Information
  • *Hiking Utah*, by Dave Hall, Falcon, 1997.
  • *Wilderness at the Edge*, by the Utah Wilderness Coalition, 1992.

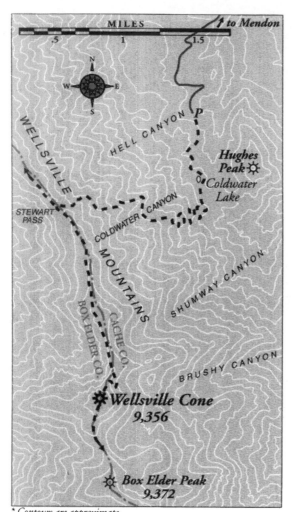

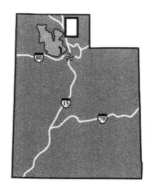

MILES

.5   1   1.5

to Mendon

N
W   E
S

WELLSVILLE

HELL CANYON

P

Hughes
Peak ☼

Coldwater
Lake

STEWART
PASS

COLDWATER CANYON

MOUNTAINS

SHUMWAY CANYON

CACHE CO.

BOX ELDER CO.

BRUSHY CANYON

☼ *Wellsville Cone*
9,356

☼ *Box Elder Peak*
9,372

* Contours are approximate

	Route
235	Secondary Road
	Dirt Road
	4WD Road
89	US Highway
15	Interstate
	Stream
▲	Campground
☼	Summit
P	Parking

to Pocatello, ID

to Preston, ID

89

15

91

BOX ELDER CO.

CACHE CO.

to
Garden
City
and
Bear Lake

BEAR RIVER RANGE

▲

30

84   Tremonton

Logan

▲

▲

P

Mendon

☼

23   89

Wellsville

WELLSVILLE MTS.

15

Brigham
City

91

CACHE CO.

RICH CO.

to Ogden

MILES

5   10   15

144

Wellsville Cone
9,356 feet

Time: 5–6 hours   4–4.5 hours

Distance: 8 miles

Difficulty: Moderate

Starting Elevation: 5,880 feet

Elevation Gain: 3,476 feet

USGS Maps: Wellsville and Honeyville

➤ Trailhead
• From Logan, drive west on 200 North (Utah Highway 30).
• Turn left/south on Utah Highway 23, following signs to Mendon and Wellsville.
• Drive 3.6 miles, passing through most of Mendon. Turn right/southwest on 1800 South.
• After a very short distance, 0.1 mile, turn right/west onto a dirt road.
• Drive 0.8 mile toward the mountains. At the Y, veer right and drive 2.4 miles to another Y. Veer right again.
• The road ends in another fraction of a mile, 3.4 miles from where the pavement ended. This is the trailhead.

(From the south end of Cache Valley, on U.S. Highway 89, turn north on Highway 23. Drive through the city of Wellsville, then the highway makes two 90-degree turns and continues on toward Mendon. After 6.7 miles from U.S. Highway 89, make a near-hairpin left/southwest turn onto 1800 South.)

➤ Camping
There are no improved campgrounds in the Wellsville Mountain Wilderness.

➤ Tips and Precautions
Avoid shortcutting the switchbacks. There is no water after Coldwater Lake. The first section of switchbacks is on a southern exposure. This can be an uncomfortable hike on a hot day.

The road approaching the trailhead is abused, misused, and getting worse. A 4-wheel-drive vehicle might be needed in the future if the Forest Service doesn't take care of the problem.

LOOKING NORTH ACROSS THE WELLSVILLES

➤ The Hike

Begin at the south side of the parking area at the signed trailhead. The trail ventures off through the dense maple forest and takes you behind Hughes Peak (the large hill between the towns of Mendon and Wellsville).

After about 0.75 mile, the easy trail comes to Coldwater Lake—actually, it's more of a pond than a lake. The trail passes to the left/east side of the lake. Be careful on the south end of the pond and don't follow the false trail toward the right/west. The trail turns slightly and drops to the left/south before continuing through the maples.

Not far after Coldwater Lake there is a junction with a trail coming up from below. Keep to the right and begin switchbacking up through the forest until you break open to the ridge. Here the terrain opens and exposes itself to the south.

The trail climbs 2,100 feet in 1.5 miles from Coldwater Lake to Stewart Pass. From here the view to the west reveals the impressive oxbow bends of the Bear River. There is often a stiff breeze on this exposed ridge.

Turning left/south at the junction on the pass, you will see two peaks along the ridge. The cone is the second peak in the distance. The trail skirts around one bump and continues along the ridge for another 1 mile before crossing over it. The trail then switchbacks up the east face of the Cone. Once the trail breaks onto the last portion of the ridge, turn left/south off the trail and hike the last 50 yards to the rounded summit.

FROM STEWART PASS, THE CONE IS IN THE BACKGROUND

➤ Background

The Wellsville Cone is Cache Valley's western landmark, a well-defined pyramid-shaped peak nesting in the center of the 22-mile-long and 5-mile-wide Wellsville Mountain range.

Although Box Elder Peak, the Cone's neighbor to the south, is 16 feet taller, we have designated the Cone a classic because of its prominence in the range and the number of hikers making it their destination.

"The range rises abruptly from 4,445 feet at the valley floor to 9,372 feet at Box Elder Peak, making it one of the steepest mountain ranges in the world," according to an early edition of *Cache Trails*.

➤ For More Information

• Wasatch-Cache National Forest, Logan Ranger District, 1500 E. Highway 89, Logan, UT 84321, (435) 755-3620.

• *Hiking Utah*, by Dave Hall, Falcon, 1997.

• *Cache Trails*, by John Wood, Bridgerland Audubon Society, 1994.

Appendix A

Equipment List

The items people carry in their packs vary widely from person to person. One person may opt to carry a full pack for one hike while another person is comfortable with just a few items shoved into their pockets for the same hike.

What someone carries is ultimately a decision that person must make based on personal experience and judgment, but it's safe to say there's a list of essential items that should always be carried.

- Map and compass
- Flashlight or headlamp, with spare bulbs and batteries
- Food
- Water
- Extra clothing—particularly for rain or foul weather
- First-aid supplies
- Pocket knife
- Matches or lighter
- Toilet paper and a plastic bag to carry used toilet paper
- Water purification (filter or chemicals)

Other items that might be added to the essentials list include sunglasses, sunscreen (for both skin and lips), a hat, and insect repellent.

Appendix B

Problems at High Altitude

Utah's county high peaks range in elevation from 9,255 feet at Rich County's unnamed peak to 13,528 feet at Kings Peak, the state's and Duchesne County's highest mountain. At those elevations, the body can be affected by a number of ailments. Those problems could be as mild as a headache, but could also be potentially fatal.

There are no specific factors such as age, gender, or physical condition that can predict altitude sickness. Some people get it and some people don't. Serious health problems are more likely if one is not accustomed, or acclimated, to high altitude. If you haven't been at high altitudes before, be cautious.

The major cause of altitude-related illnesses is going too high too fast. Given time, your body can adapt to the decrease in oxygen at higher elevations. Acclimatization is affected by dehydration, over-exertion, alcohol, and other depressant drugs.

Perhaps the most common of high altitude illnesses, Acute Mountain Sickness, strikes to some degree 75 percent of people who climb to elevations above 10,000 feet. Symptoms include headache, dizziness, fatigue, shortness of breath, loss of appetite, nausea, disturbed sleep, and a general sick feeling. The symptoms tend to get worse at night when respirations decrease. In most mild cases, those symptoms will subside in 2 to 3 days. As long as the symptoms remain mild, it's generally safe to continue climbing at a moderate rate. However, if the symptoms get worse, it's best to descend until you get better acclimated. Even a few hundred of feet of descending can lead to remarkable signs of improvement.

Moderate AMS will include a bad headache, nausea and vomiting, increased weakness and fatigue, shortness of breath, and ataxia (decreased co-ordination). Normal activity will be difficult, but you may still be able to walk on your own. If these symptoms get worse, including an inability to walk or shortness of breath at rest, immediate descent to a lower elevation is necessary.

There are two other forms of severe altitude illness: High Altitude Pulmonary Edema and High Altitude Cerebral Edema.

High Altitude Pulmonary Edema (HAPE) results from fluid building up in the lungs. This can lead to cyanosis, impaired cerebral function, and death. Symptoms include shortness of breath at rest, a tight feeling in the chest, fatigue, a feeling of impending suffocation at night, weakness, and a persistent cough that produces a white frothy fluid. Confusion and irrational behavior are common among people afflicted with HAPE.

High Altitude Cerebral Edema (HACE) is the result of brain tissue swelling from fluid leakage. Symptoms can include headache, ataxia, weakness, and decreased levels of consciousness—disorientation, memory loss, hallucinations, psychotic behavior, and coma. HACE usually doesn't occur until after a week at high altitude.

People suffering from HAPE or HACE must descend from high altitudes and seek professional care at a medical facility.

While there are some drugs that may reduce the susceptibility to high altitude illnesses, they are probably not necessary for climbing Utah's county high peaks.

SCOTT DUNN TAKES A BREAK ON THE WAY TO MOUNT NEBO

Selected Readings

Abbey, Edward, *The Monkey Wrench Gang*, Dream Garden Press, 1985.

Biddle, M., *Fishlake National Forest Backcountry Guide for Hiking and Horseback Riding*, Wasatch, 1993.

Camping and Picnicking in the National Forests of Utah, U.S. Forest Service, 1995.

Daffern, Tony, *Avalanche Safety for Skiers and Climbers*, Alpenbooks, 1985.

Davis, Mel, and John Veranth, *High Uinta Trails*, Wasatch, 1993.

Forgey, William, *Wilderness Medical Society Practice Guidelines for Wilderness Emergency Care*, ICS Books, 1995.

Hackett, Peter, *Mountain Sickness: Prevention, Recognition and Treatment*, American Alpine Club, 1984.

Hall, Dave, *Hiking Utah*, formerly *The Hiker's Guide to Utah*, Falcon, 1997.

Huff, Paula, and Tom Wharton, *Hiking Utah's Summits*, Falcon, 1997 (a compilation of a series of articles that first appeared in *The Salt Lake Tribune*).

Kelsey, Michael, *Hiking and Exploring Utah's Henry Mountains and Robber's Roost*, Kelsey Publishing Co., 1987.

———.*Climbing and Exploring Utah's Mt. Timpanogos*, Kelsey Publishing Co., 1989.

———.*Utah Mountaineering Guide*, Kelsey Publishing Co., 1997.

Knighton, José, *Canyon Country's La Sal Mountains Hiking and Nature Handbook*, Canyon Country, 1995.

Leopold, Aldo, *A Sand County Almanac*, Commemorative Edition, Oxford University Press, 1987.

Mountaineering: The Freedom of the Hills, The Mountaineers, 1992.

Nichols, Gary C., *Trails of The Wasatch, A Pocket Guide*, Nichols, 1996.

Paxman, Shirley and Monroe, and Gayle and Weldon Taylor, *Utah Valley Trails*, Wasatch, 1978.

Turner, Jack, *The Abstract Wild*, University of Arizona Press, 1996.

Van Cott, John W., *Utah Place Names*, University of Utah Press, 1990.

Veranth, John, *Hiking the Wasatch*, Wasatch Mountain Club, 1988.

Wilderness at the Edge, The Utah Wilderness Coalition, 1992.

Wilkerson, James, ed., *Medicine For Mountaineering & Other Wilderness Activities*, The Mountaineers, 1992.

Wood, John, *Cache Trails*, Bridgerland Audubon Society, 1994.

Acknowledgments

Sincere thanks to Jeff Grathwohl and Rodger Reynolds of the University of Utah Press for their help and support. Jeff liked our idea from the start and was willing to go to bat for us.

Dozens of people joined us on various hikes throughout the state. While we can't name all of them, thanks go out to Kevin Brewer, Scott Dunn, Mark Elzey, Stanley Holmes, Wesley Holmes, José Knighton, Kandi Kutkas, Marlin Stum, Rory Tyler, and S. John Wilkin.

Knighton's experience in the La Sal Mountains was also invaluable, especially in helping us find a route to Mount Waas that didn't pass through private property.

Elzey's biology background was beneficial, too, in helping us gain an understanding of the flora and fauna of Utah's county high peaks. Three Logan High School students tried to help us with the plants and animals chapter, but in the end we used information that was generously provided by Bicycle Utah Vacation Guides, Inc.

Dunn also helped proofread our manuscript—working as late as 3 A.M. to help us meet our deadline.

Utah's mountain weather couldn't be better explained by anyone other than William Alder, the chief meteorologist for the National Weather Service office in Salt Lake City.

Diane Fouts deserves credit for wading through Dan's preface and making a photojournalist's prose more readable.

Scott Wyatt gave us the idea but unfortunately his work and family schedule didn't allow him time to join us on any hikes.

Evan Hanson, who climbed all of Utah's county high peaks with his son Ty during the same summer, shared tales of their adventures and compared notes with us when we were done.

Most of all, we want to thank our families for putting up with us during this project and offering support when it was needed most. Dan's wife, Diane Bush, joined us for many of the hikes and helped provide some of the photographs for this book. Mike's new bride, Lora Wight, helped proofread the manuscript, and she corrected many of the mistakes even the computer's spell check had missed. Lora and her three kids, Ben, Mike, and Jenny Knoll, were patient even when tensions ran high while planning a wedding and trying to get all of our hiking done before the first snow.

About The Authors

 Michael R. Weibel

Mike is a native San Diegan who moved to the Midwest in 1982 to study journalism at the University of Nebraska. After graduating with a bachelor's degree in 1987, he worked for newspapers in Oklahoma and Nebraska before moving to Utah in 1992. He is the senior reporter at *The Herald Journal* in Logan where he has worked for seven years. He enjoys the occasional opportunity to hike, climb, and ski. He has also contributed to *Rock & Ice Online* magazine as a regional correspondent for Northern Utah. He is married to Lora Wight and they live in Hyde Park, Utah.

Dan Miller

Dan has been a photographer in Utah since 1979. He began his career doing several pieces for *Utah Holiday* magazine and working for the *Lakeside Review*, a weekly newspaper in Utah's Davis County. He moved to Salt Lake City where he worked for five years at *The Salt Lake Tribune*. During his time there, he shot photographs for the book *Utah! A Family Travel Guide*. In 1989, he moved to Logan, Utah, where he worked for seven years at *The Herald Journal*—three years as the newspaper's photo editor. He is a freelance photographer and stringer for *Salt Lake* magazine in Salt Lake City and a contributing editor for *Edging West* magazine in Portland, Oregon. He has been published in Sports Illustrated, Life, The Ancorage Daily News and The Seattle Times. His photography is also featured in *Visions of Antelope Island and Great Salt Lake* due out in Spring, 1999. He is married to Diane Bush, a photographer and great hiker.